COMPUTER
SCIENCE
DISTILLED

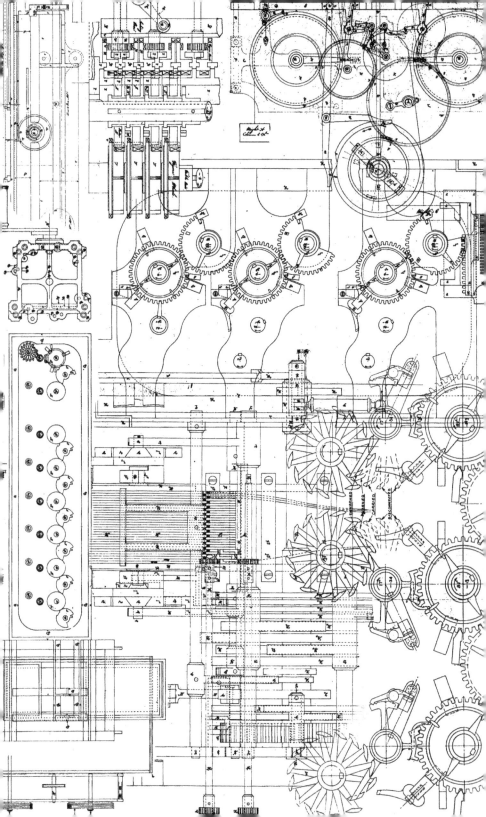

COMPUTER SCIENCE
DISTILLED

LEARN THE ART OF SOLVING
COMPUTATIONAL PROBLEMS

WLADSTON FERREIRA FILHO

code energy

Las Vegas

Edited by Raimondo Pictet.

Published by CODE ENERGY LLC

✉ hi@code.energy
🖥 http://code.energy
🐦 http://twitter.com/code_energy
👍 http://facebook.com/code.energy
🏠 304 S Jones Blvd # 401 Las Vegas NV 89107 ▦

While every precaution has been taken in the preparation of this book, the publisher and the author assume no responsibility for errors or omissions, or for damages resulting from the use of the information contained herein.

Publisher's Cataloging-in-Publication Data
Ferreira Filho, Wladston.
    Computer science distilled: learn the art of solving computational problems / Wladston Viana Ferreira Filho. — 1st ed.
    x, 168 p. : il.
    ISBN 978-0-9973160-2-5
    eISBN 978-0-9973160-1-8
1. Computer algorithms. 2. Computer programming. 3. Computer science. 4. Data structures (Computer science). I. Title.
004 – dc22   2016909247

First Edition, December 2018.

Friends are the family we choose for ourselves. This book is dedicated to my friends Rômulo, Léo, Moto and Chris, who kept pushing me to "finish the damn book already".

I know that two & two make four—and should be glad to prove it too if I could—though I must say if by any sort of process I could convert 2 & 2 into *five* it would give me much greater pleasure.

—LORD BYRON
1813 letter to his future wife Annabella.
Their daughter Ada Lovelace was the first programmer.

CONTENTS

PREFACE

> Everybody in this country should learn to program a computer, because it teaches you how to think.
>
> —STEVE JOBS

As computers changed the world with their unprecedented power, a new science flourished: *computer science*. It showed how computers could be used to solve problems. It allowed us to push machines to their full potential. And we achieved crazy, amazing things.

Computer science is everywhere, but it's still taught as boring theory. Many coders never even study it! However, computer science is crucial to effective programming. Some friends of mine simply can't find a good coder to hire. Computing power is abundant, but people who can use it are scarce.

This is my humble attempt to help the world, by pushing *you* to use computers efficiently. This book presents computer science concepts in their plain distilled forms. I will keep academic formalities to a minimum. Hopefully, computer science will stick to your mind and improve your code.

Figure 1   "Computer Problems", courtesy of http://xkcd.com.

Is this book for me?

If you want to smash problems with efficient solutions, this book is for you. Little programming experience is required. If you already wrote a few lines of code and recognize basic programming statements like `for` and `while`, you'll be OK. If not, online programming courses[1] cover more than what's required. You can do one in a week, for free. For those who studied computer science, this book is an excellent recap for consolidating your knowledge.

But isn't computer science just for academics?

This book is for everyone. It's about *computational thinking*. You'll learn to change problems into computable systems. You'll use computational thinking on everyday problems. Prefetching and caching will streamline your packing. Parallelism will speed up your cooking. Plus, your code will be awesome. 😌

May the force be with you,
Wlad

---

[1]http://code.energy/coding-courses.

CHAPTER 1

Basics

> Computer science is not about machines, in the same way that astronomy is not about telescopes. There is an essential unity of mathematics and computer science.
>
> —EDSGER DIJKSTRA

COMPUTERS NEED US to break down problems into chunks they can crunch. To do this, we need some math. Don't panic, it's not rocket science—writing good code rarely calls for complicated equations. This chapter is just a toolbox for problem solving. You'll learn to:

- Model **ideas** into flowcharts and pseudocode,
- ✔ Know right from wrong with **logic**,
- 100 **Count** stuff,
- Calculate **probabilities** safely.

With this, you will have what it takes to translate your ideas into computable solutions.

1.1 Ideas

When you're on a complex task, keep your brain at the top of its game: dump all important stuff on paper. Our brains' working memory easily overflows with facts and ideas. Writing everything down is part of many organizing methods. There are several ways to do it. We'll first see how flowcharts are used to represent processes. We'll then learn how programmable processes can be drafted in pseudocode. We'll also try and model a simple problem with math.

1

Flowcharts

When Wikipedians discussed their collaboration process, they created a flowchart that was updated as the debate progressed. Having a picture of what was being proposed helped the discussion:

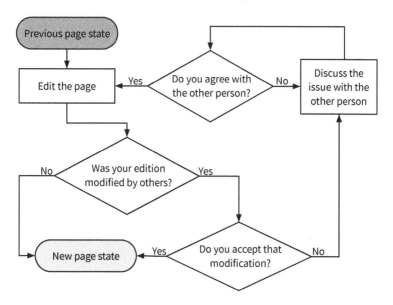

Figure 1.1   Wiki edition process (adapted from http://wikipedia.org).

Like the editing process above, computer code is essentially a process. Programmers often use flowcharts for writing down computing processes. When doing so, you should follow these guidelines[1] for others to understand your flowcharts:

- Write states and instruction steps inside rectangles.
- Write decision steps, where the process may go different ways, inside diamonds.
- Never mix an instruction step with a decision step.
- Connect sequential steps with arrows.
- Mark the start and end of the process.

---

[1]There's even an ISO standard specifying precisely how software systems diagrams should be drawn, called **UML**: http://code.energy/UML.

Let's see how this works for finding the biggest of three numbers:

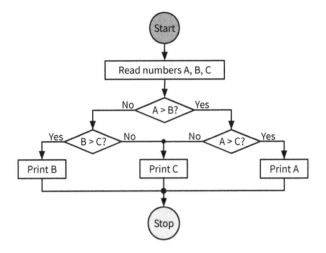

Figure 1.2   Finding the maximum value between three variables.

Pseudocode

Just as flowcharts, **pseudocode** expresses computational processes. Pseudocode is human-friendly code that cannot be understood by a machine. The following example is the same as fig. 1.2. Take a minute and test it out with some sample values of A, B, and C:[2]

```
function maximum(A, B, C)
    if A > B
        if A > C
            max ← A
        else
            max ← C
    else
        if B > C
            max ← B
        else
            max ← C
    print max
```

---

[2]Here, ← is the assignment operator: x ← 1 reads *x is set to 1.*

Notice how this example completely disregards the syntactic rules of programming languages? When you write pseudocode, you can even throw in some spoken language! Just as you use flowcharts to compose general mind maps, let your creativity flow free when writing pseudocode (fig. 1.3 ☺).

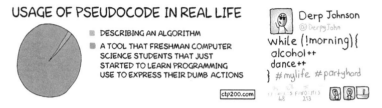

Figure 1.3 "Pseudocode in Real Life", courtesy of http://ctp200.com.

Mathematical Models

A **model** is a set of concepts that represents a problem and its characteristics. It allows us to better reason and operate with the problem. Creating models is so important it's taught in school. High school math is (or should be) about modeling problems into numbers and equations, and applying tools on those to reach a solution.

Mathematically described models have a great advantage: they can be adapted for computers using well established math techniques. If your model has graphs, use graph theory. If it has equations, use algebra. *Stand on the shoulders of giants* who created these tools. It will do the trick. Let's see that in action in a typical high school problem:

> LIVESTOCK FENCE 🐑🐖 Your farm has two types of livestock. You have 100 units of barbed wire to make a rectangular fence for the animals, with a straight division for separating them. How do you frame the fence in order to maximize the pasture's area?

Starting with what's to be determined, w and l are the pasture's dimensions; $w \times l$, the area. Maximizing it means using all the barbed wire, so we relate w and l with 100:

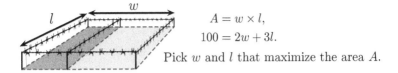

$$A = w \times l,$$
$$100 = 2w + 3l.$$

Pick w and l that maximize the area A.

Plugging l from the second equation ($l = \frac{100-2w}{3}$) into the first,

$$A = \frac{100}{3}w - \frac{2}{3}w^2.$$

That's a quadratic equation! Its maximum is easily found with the high school *quadratic formula*. Set $A = 0$, solve the equation, and the maximum is the midway point between the two roots. Quadratic equations are important for you as a pressure cooking pot is valuable to cooks. They save time. Quadratic equations help us solve many problems faster. Remember, your duty is to solve problems. A cook knows his tools, you should know yours. You need mathematical modeling. And you will need logic.

1.2 Logic

Coders work with logic *so much* it messes their minds. Still, many coders don't really learn logic and use it unknowingly. By learning formal logic, we can deliberately use it to solve problems.

Figure 1.4 "Programmer's Logic", courtesy of http://programmers.life.

We will start playing around with logical statements using special operators and special algebra. We'll then learn to solve problems with truth tables and see how computers rely on logic.

Operators

In common math, variables and operators ($+$, $\times$, $-$,...) are used to model numerical problems. In mathematical logic, variables and operators represent the validity of things. They don't express numbers, but `True`/`False` values. For instance, the validity of the expression *"if the pool is warm, I'll swim"* is based on the validity of two things, which can be mapped to **logical variables** A and B:

> A : The pool is warm.
>
> B : I swim.

They're either `True` or `False`.[3] $A =$ `True` means a warm pool; $B =$ `False` means no swimming. B can't be *half-true*, because I can't half swim. Dependency between variables is expressed with $\rightarrow$, the **conditional operator**. $A \rightarrow B$ is the idea that $A =$ `True` implies $B =$ `True`:

> $A \rightarrow B$: If the pool is warm, then I'll swim.

With more operators, different ideas can be expressed. To negate ideas, we use $!$, the **negation operator**. $!A$ is the opposite of A:

> $!A$: The pool is cold.
>
> $!B$: I don't swim.

THE CONTRAPOSITIVE Given $A \rightarrow B$ and I didn't swim, what can be said about the pool? A warm pool *forces* the swimming, so without swimming, it's impossible for the pool to be warm. Every conditional expression has a **contrapositive** equivalent:

> for any two variables A and B,
>
> $A \rightarrow B$ is the same as $!B \rightarrow !A$.

---

[3]Values can be in between in fuzzy logic, but it won't be covered in this book.

Another example: *if you can't write good code, you haven't read this book.* Its contrapositive is *if you read this book, you can write good code.* Both sentences say the same in different ways.[4]

THE BICONDITIONAL Be careful, saying *"if the pool is warm, I'll swim"* doesn't mean I'll only swim in warm water. The statement promises nothing about cold pools. In other words, $A \rightarrow B$ doesn't mean $B \rightarrow A$. To express both conditionals, use the **biconditional**:

$A \leftrightarrow B$: I'll swim if and only if the pool is warm.

Here, the pool being warm is equivalent to me swimming: knowing about the pool means knowing if I'll swim *and vice-versa.* Again, beware of the **inverse error**: never presume $B \rightarrow A$ follows from $A \rightarrow B$.

AND, OR, EXCLUSIVE OR These logical operators are the most famous, as they're often explicitly coded. AND expresses all ideas are True; OR expresses any idea is True; XOR expresses ideas are of opposing truths. Imagine a party serving vodka and wine:

A : You drank wine. 🍷

B : You drank vodka. 🍸

A OR B : You drank. 🎉

A AND B : You drank mixing drinks. 🥴

A XOR B : You drank without mixing. 😌

Make sure you understand how the operators we've seen so far work. The following table recaps all possible combinations for two variables. Notice how $A \rightarrow B$ is equivalent to $!A$ OR B, and A XOR B is equivalent to $!(A \leftrightarrow B)$.

---

[4]And by the way, 😉 they're both *actually* true.

Table 1.1 Logical operations for 4 possible values of A and B.

A	B	$!A$	$A \to B$	$A \leftrightarrow B$	A AND B	A OR B	A XOR B
✓	✓	✗	✓	✓	✓	✓	✗
✓	✗	✗	✗	✗	✗	✓	✓
✗	✓	✓	✓	✗	✗	✓	✓
✗	✗	✓	✓	✓	✗	✗	✗

Boolean Algebra

As elementary algebra simplifies numerical expressions, **boolean algebra**[5] simplifies logical expressions.

ASSOCIATIVITY Parentheses are irrelevant for sequences of AND or OR operations. As sequences of sums or multiplications in elementary algebra, they can be calculated in any order.

$$A \text{ AND } (B \text{ AND } C) = (A \text{ AND } B) \text{ AND } C.$$
$$A \text{ OR } (B \text{ OR } C) = (A \text{ OR } B) \text{ OR } C.$$

DISTRIBUTIVITY In elementary algebra we factor multiplicative terms from sums: $a \times (b + c) = (a \times b) + (a \times c)$. Likewise in logic, ANDing after an OR is equivalent to ORing results of ANDs, and vice versa:

$$A \text{ AND } (B \text{ OR } C) = (A \text{ AND } B) \text{ OR } (A \text{ AND } C).$$
$$A \text{ OR } (B \text{ AND } C) = (A \text{ OR } B) \text{ AND } (A \text{ OR } C).$$

DEMORGAN'S LAW[6] It can't be summer *and* winter at once, so it's either *not* summer *or not* winter. And it's not summer and not winter *if and only if* it's *not* the case it's either summer *or* winter. Following this reasoning, ANDs can be transformed into ORs and vice versa:

---

[5]After George Boole. His 1854 book joined logic and math, starting all this.

[6]De Morgan was friends with Boole. He tutored the young Ada Lovelace, who became the first programmer a century before the first computer was constructed.

$$!(A \text{ AND } B) = \,!A \text{ OR } !B,$$
$$!A \text{ AND } !B = \,!(A \text{ OR } B).$$

These rules transform logical models, reveal properties, and simplify expressions. Let's solve a problem:

> Hot Server ✵ A server crashes if it's overheating while the air conditioning is off. It also crashes if it's overheating and its chassis cooler fails. In which conditions does the server work?

Modeling it in logical variables, the conditions for the server to crash can be stated in a single expression:

A : Server overheats.
B : Air conditioning off.
C : Chassis cooler fails.
D : Server crashes.

$$(A \text{ AND } B) \text{ OR } (A \text{ AND } C) \to D.$$

Using distributivity, we factorize the expression:

$$A \text{ AND } (B \text{ OR } C) \to D.$$

The server works when $(!D)$. The contrapositive reads:

$$!D \to \,!(A \text{ AND } (B \text{ OR } C)).$$

We use DeMorgan's Law to remove parentheses:

$$!D \to \,!A \text{ OR } !(B \text{ OR } C).$$

Applying DeMorgan's Law again,

$$!D \to \,!A \text{ OR } (!B \text{ AND } !C).$$

This expression tells us that whenever the server works, either $!A$ (it's not overheating), or $!B$ AND $!C$ (both air conditioning *and* chassis cooler are working).

Truth Tables

Another way to analyze logical models is checking what happens in all possible configurations of its variables. A **truth table** has a column for each variable. Rows represent possible combinations of variable states.

One variable requires two rows: in one the variable is set `True`, in the other `False`. To add a variable, we duplicate the rows. We set the new variable `True` in the original rows, and `False` in the duplicated rows (fig. 1.5). The truth table size doubles for each added variable, so it can only be constructed for a few variables.[7]

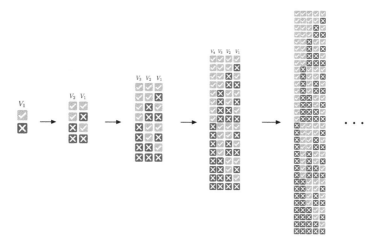

Figure 1.5 Tables listing the configurations of 1–5 logical variables.

Let's see how a truth table can be used to analyze a problem.

FRAGILE SYSTEM 🖥 We have to create a database system with the following requirements:

    I : If the database is locked, we can save data.
    II : A database lock on a full write queue cannot happen.
    III : Either the write queue is full, or the cache is loaded.
    IV : If the cache is loaded, the database cannot be locked.

Is this possible? Under which conditions will it work?

---

[7]A truth table for 30 variables would have more than a billion rows. ▮

First we transform each requirement into a logical expression. This database system can be modeled using four variables:

A : Database is locked.　　　I : $A \to B$.
B : Able to save data.　　　II : $!(A$ AND $C)$.
C : Write queue is full.　　　III : C OR D.
D : Cache is loaded.　　　IV : $D \to !A$.

We then create a truth table with all possible configurations. Extra columns are added to check the requirements.

Table 1.2　Truth table for exploring the validity of four expressions.

State #	A	B	C	D	I	II	III	IV	All four
1	✗	✗	✗	✗	✓	✓	✗	✓	✗
2	✗	✗	✗	✓	✓	✓	✓	✓	✓
3	✗	✗	✓	✗	✓	✓	✓	✓	✓
4	✗	✗	✓	✓	✓	✓	✓	✓	✓
5	✗	✓	✗	✗	✓	✓	✗	✓	✗
6	✗	✓	✗	✓	✓	✓	✓	✓	✓
7	✗	✓	✓	✗	✓	✓	✓	✓	✓
8	✗	✓	✓	✓	✓	✓	✓	✓	✓
9	✓	✗	✗	✗	✗	✓	✗	✓	✗
10	✓	✗	✗	✓	✗	✓	✓	✗	✗
11	✓	✗	✓	✗	✗	✗	✓	✓	✗
12	✓	✗	✓	✓	✗	✗	✓	✗	✗
13	✓	✓	✗	✗	✓	✓	✗	✓	✗
14	✓	✓	✗	✓	✓	✓	✓	✗	✗
15	✓	✓	✓	✗	✓	✗	✓	✓	✗
16	✓	✓	✓	✓	✓	✗	✓	✗	✗

All requirements are met in states 2–4 and 6–8. In these states, $A =$ False, meaning the database can't ever be locked. Notice the cache will not be loaded only in states 3 and 7.

To test what you've learned, solve the Zebra Puzzle.[8] It's a famous logic problem wrongly attributed to Einstein. They say only 2% of people can solve it, but I doubt that. Using a big truth table and correctly simplifying and combining logic statements, I'm sure you'll crack it.

Whenever you're dealing with things that assume one of two possibilities, remember they can be modeled as logic variables. This way, it's easy to derive expressions, simplify them, and draw conclusions. Let's now see the most impressive application of logic: the design of electronic computers.

Logic in Computing

Groups of logical variables can represent numbers in binary form.[9] Logic operations on binary digits can be combined to perform general calculations. **Logic gates** perform logic operations on electric current. They are used in electrical circuits that can perform calculations at very high speeds.

A logic gate receives values through input wires, performs its operation, and places the result on its output wire. There are AND gates, OR gates, XOR gates, and more. True and False are represented by electric currents with high or low voltage. Using gates, complex logical expressions can be computed near instantly. For example, this electrical circuit sums two numbers:

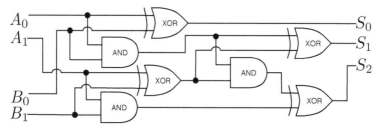

Figure 1.6 A circuit to sum 2-bit numbers given by pairs of logical variables ($A_1 A_0$ and $B_1 B_0$) into a 3-bit number ($S_2 S_1 S_0$).

---

[8]http://code.energy/zebra-puzzle.

[9]True $= 1$, False $= 0$. If you have no idea why 101 in binary represents the number 5, check Appendix I for an explanation of number systems.

Let's see how this circuit works. Take a minute to follow the operations performed by the circuit to realize how the magic happens:

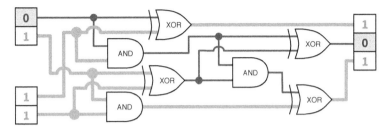

Figure 1.7 Calculating $2 + 3 = 5$ (in binary, $10 + 11 = 101$).

To take advantage of this fast form of computing, we transform numerical problems to their binary/logical form. Truth tables help model and test circuits. Boolean algebra simplifies expressions and thus simplifies circuits.

At first, gates were made with bulky, inefficient and expensive electrical valves. Once valves were replaced with transistors, logic gates could be produced en masse. And we kept discovering ways to make transistors smaller and smaller.[10] The working principles of the modern CPU are still based on boolean algebra. A modern CPU is just a circuit of millions of microscopic wires and logic gates that manipulate electric currents of information.

1.3   Counting

It's important to count things correctly—you'll have to do it many times when working with computational problems.[11] The math in this section will be more complex, but don't be scared. Some people think they can't be good coders because they think they're bad at math. Well, I failed high school math 😖, yet here I am 😄. The math that makes a good coder is not what's required in typical math exams from schools.

---

[10]In 2016, researchers created working transistors on a 1 nm scale. For reference, a gold *atom* is 0.15 nm wide.

[11]**Counting** and **Logic** belong to an important field to computer science called **Discrete Mathematics**.

Outside school, formulas and step-by-step procedures aren't memorized. They are looked up on the Internet when needed. Calculations mustn't be in pen and paper. What a good coder requires is intuition. Learning about counting problems will strengthen that intuition. Let's now grind through a bunch of tools step by step: multiplications, permutations, combinations and sums.

Multiplying

If an event happens in n different ways, and another event happens in m different ways, the number of different ways both events can happen is $n \times m$. For example:

CRACKING THE CODE 🔐   A PIN code is composed of two digits and a letter. It takes one second to try a PIN. In the worst case, how much time do we need to crack a PIN?

Two digits can be chosen in 100 ways (00-99) and a letter in 26 ways (A-Z). Therefore, there are $100 \times 26 = 2,600$ possible PINs. In the worst case, we have to try every single PIN until we find the right one. After 2,600 seconds (43 minutes), we'll have cracked it.

TEAM BUILDING 👥   There are 23 candidates who want to join your team. For each candidate, you toss a coin and only hire if it shows heads. How many team configurations are possible?

Before hiring, the only possible team configuration is you alone. Each coin toss then doubles the number of possible configurations. This has to be done 23 times, so we compute 2 *to the power 23*:

$$\underbrace{2 \times 2 \times \cdots \times 2}_{23 \text{ times}} = 2^{23} = 8,388,608 \text{ team configurations.}$$

Note that one of these configurations is still you alone.

Permutations

If we have n items, we can order them in n factorial ($n!$) different ways. The factorial is explosive, it gets to enormous numbers for small values of n. If you are not familiar,

$$n! = n \times (n-1) \times (n-2) \times \cdots \times 2 \times 1.$$

It's easy to see $n!$ is the number of ways n items can be ordered. In how many ways can you choose a first item among n? After the first item was chosen, in how many ways can you choose a second one? Afterwards, how many options are left for a third? Think about it, then we'll move on to more examples.[12]

TRAVELING SALESMAN 🚚 Your truck company delivers to 15 cities. You want to know in what order to serve these cities to minimize gas consumption. If it takes a microsecond to calculate the length of one route, how long does it take to compute the length of all possible routes?

Each permutation of the 15 cities is a different route. The factorial is the number of distinct permutations, so there are $15! = 15 \times 14 \times \cdots \times 1 \approx 1.3$ trillion routes. That in microseconds is roughly equivalent to 15 days. If instead you had 20 cities, it would take *77 thousand years*.

THE PRECIOUS TUNE 🎼 A musician is studying a scale with 13 different notes. She wants you to render all possible melodies that use six notes only. Each note should play once per melody, and each six-note melody should play for one second. How much audio runtime is she asking for?

We want to count permutations of six out of the 13 notes. To ignore permutations of unused notes, we must stop developing the factorial after the sixth factor. Formally, $n!/(n-m)!$ is the number of possible permutations of m out of n possible items. In our case:

---

[12]By convention, $0! = 1$. We say there's one way to order zero items.

$$\frac{13!}{(13-6)!} = \frac{13 \times 12 \times 11 \times 10 \times 9 \times 8 \times 7!}{7!}$$

$$= \underbrace{13 \times 12 \times 11 \times 10 \times 9 \times 8}_{\text{6 factors}}$$

$$= 1,235,520 \text{ melodies.}$$

That's over 1.2 million one-second melodies—it would take 343 hours to listen to everything. Better convince the musician to find the perfect melody some other way.

Permutations with Identical Items

The factorial $n!$ overcounts the number of ways to order n items if some are identical. Identical items swapping their positions shouldn't count as a different permutation.

In a sequence of n items of which r are identical, there are $r!$ ways to reorder identical items. Thus, $n!$ counts each distinct permutation $r!$ times. To get the number of distinct permutations, we need to divide $n!$ by this overcount factor. For instance, the number of distinct permutations of the letters "CODE ENERGY" is $10!/3!$.

PLAYING WITH DNA 🎲 A biologist is studying a DNA segment related to a genetic disease. The segment is made of 23 base pairs, where 9 must be A-T, 14 must be G-C. She wants to run a simulation task on every possible DNA segment having these numbers of base pairs. How many simulation tasks is she looking at?

First we calculate all possible permutations of the 23 base pairs. Then we divide the result to account for the 9 repeated A-T and the 14 repeated G-C base pairs:

$$23!/(9! \times 14!) = 817,190 \text{ base pair permutations.}$$

But the problem isn't over. Considering orientation of base pairs:

 isn't the same as

For each sequence of 23 base pairs, there are 2^{23} distinct orientation configurations. Therefore, the total is:

$$817,190 \times 2^{23} \approx 7 \text{ trillion sequences.}$$

And that's for a tiny 23 base pair sequence with a known distribution. The smallest replicable DNA known so far are from the minuscule *Porcine circovirus*, and it has 1,800 base pairs! DNA code and life are truly amazing from a technological point of view. It's crazy: human DNA has about 3 billion base pairs, replicated in each of the 3 trillion cells of the human body.

Combinations

Picture a deck of 13 cards containing all ♠ spades. How many ways can you deal six cards to your opponent? We've seen $13!/(13 - 6)!$ is the number of permutations of six out of 13 possible items. Since the order of the six cards doesn't matter, we must divide this by $6!$ to obtain:

$$\frac{13!}{6!(13 - 6)!} = 1,716 \text{ combinations.}$$

The binomial $\binom{n}{m}$ is the number of ways to select m items out of a set of n items, regardless of order:

$$\binom{n}{m} = \frac{n!}{m!(n - m)!}.$$

The binomial is read "n choose m".

CHESS QUEENS ♛ You have an empty chessboard and 8 queens, which can be placed anywhere on the board. In how many different ways can the queens be placed?

The chessboard has 64 squares in an 8×8 grid. The number of ways to choose 8 squares out of the available 64 is $\binom{64}{8} \approx 4.4$ billion.[13]

Sums

Calculating sums of sequences occurs often when counting. Sequential sums are expressed using the **capital-sigma** (Σ) notation. It indicates how an expression will be summed for each value of i:

$$\sum_{\text{start } i}^{\text{finish } i} \text{expression of } i.$$

For instance, summing the first five odd numbers is written:

$$\sum_{i=0}^{4}(2i + 1) = 1 + 3 + 5 + 7 + 9.$$

Note i was replaced by each number between 0 and 4 to obtain 1, 3, 5, 7 and 9. Summing the first n natural numbers is thus:

$$\sum_{i=1}^{n} i = 1 + 2 + \cdots + (n - 1) + n.$$

When the prodigious mathematician Gauss was ten years old, he got tired of summing natural numbers one by one and found this neat trick:

$$\sum_{i=1}^{n} i = \frac{n(n + 1)}{2}.$$

Can you guess how Gauss discovered this? The trick is explained in Appendix II. Let's see how we can use it to solve a problem:

FLYING CHEAP ✈ You need to fly to New York City anytime in the next 30 days. Air ticket prices change unpredictably according to the departure *and* return dates. How many pairs of days must be checked to find the cheapest tickets for flying to NYC and back within the next 30 days?

---

[13] Pro tip: Google `64 choose 8` for the result.

Any pair of days between today (day 1) and the last day (day 30) is valid, as long as the return is the same day of later than the departure. Hence, 30 pairs begin with day 1, 29 pairs begin with day 2, 28 with day 3, and so on. There's only one pair that begins on day 30. So 30+29+...+2+1 is the total number of pairs that needs to be considered. We can write this $\sum_{i=1}^{30} i$ and use our handy formula:

$$\sum_{i=1}^{30} i = \frac{30(30+1)}{2} = 465 \text{ pairs.}$$

Also, we can solve this using combinations. From the 30 days available, pick two. The order doesn't matter: the earlier day is the departure, the later day is the return. This gives $\binom{30}{2} = 435$. But wait! We must count the cases where arrival and departure are the same date. There are 30 such cases, thus $\binom{30}{2} + 30 = 465$.

1.4 Probability

The principles of randomness will help you understand gambling, forecast the weather, or design a backup system with low risk of failure. The principles are simple, yet misunderstood by most people.

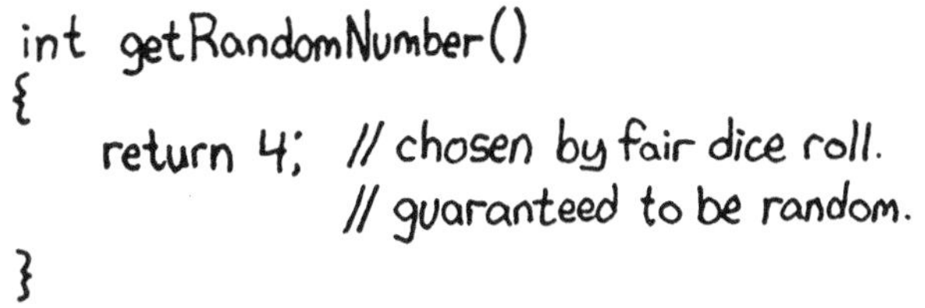

```
int getRandomNumber()
{
    return 4; // chosen by fair dice roll.
              // guaranteed to be random.
}
```

Figure 1.8 "Random number", courtesy of http://xkcd.com.

Let's start using our counting skills to compute odds. Then we'll learn how different event types are used to solve problems. Finally, we'll see why gamblers lose everything.

Counting Outcomes

A die roll has six possible outcomes: ⚀, ⚁, ⚂, ⚃, ⚄ and ⚅. The chances of getting ⚃ are thus 1/6. How about getting an odd number? It can happen in three ways (⚀, ⚂ or ⚄), so the chances are $3/6 = 1/2$. Formally, the **probability** of an event to occur is:

$$P(\text{event}) = \frac{\#\text{ of ways event can happen}}{\#\text{ of possible outcomes}}.$$

This works because each possible outcome is equally likely to happen: the die is well balanced and the thrower isn't cheating.

> TEAM BUILDING, AGAIN 👤 There are 23 candidates who want to join your team. For each candidate, you toss a coin and only hire if it shows heads. What are the chances of hiring nobody?

We've seen there are $2^{23} = 8,388,608$ possible team configurations. The only way to hire nobody is by tossing 23 consecutive tails. The probability of that happening is thus $P(\text{nobody}) = 1/8,388,608$. To put things into perspective, the probability that a given commercial airline flight crashes is about one in five million.

Independent Events

If you toss a coin and roll a die, the chance of getting heads and ⚅ is $1/2 \times 1/6 = 1/12 \approx 0.08$, or 8%. When the outcome of an event does not influence the outcome of another event, they are **independent**. The probability that two independent events will happen is the product of their individual probabilities.

> BACKING UP 💾 You need to store data for a year. One disk has a probability of failing of one in a billion. Another disk costs 20% the price but has a probability of failing of one in two thousand. What should you buy?

If you use three cheap disks, you only lose the data if all three disks fail. The probability of that happening is $(1/2,000)^3 = 1/8,000,000,000$. This redundancy achieves a lower risk of data loss than the expensive disk, while costing only 60% the price.

Mutually Exclusive Events

A die roll cannot simultaneously yield ⸭ and an odd number. The probability to get either ⸭ or an odd number is thus $1/6 + 1/2 = 2/3$. When two events cannot happen simultaneously, they are **mutually exclusive**. If you need any of the mutually exclusive events to happen, just sum their individual probabilities.

> SUBSCRIPTION CHOICE ✅ Your website offers three plans: free, basic, or pro. You know a random new customer has a probability of 70% of choosing the free plan, 20% for the basic, and 10% for the pro. What are the chances a new user will sign up for a paying plan?

The events are mutually exclusive: a user can't choose *both* the basic and pro plans at the same time. The probability the user will pay is $0.2 + 0.1 = 0.3$.

Complementary Events

A die roll cannot simultaneously yield a multiple of three (⸭, ⸭) and a number *not* divisible by three, but it must yield one of them. The probability to get a multiple of three is $2/6 = 1/3$, so the probability to get a number *not* divisible by three is $1 - 1/3 = 2/3$. When two mutually exclusive events cover all possible outcomes, they are **complementary**. The sum of individual probabilities of complementary events is thus 100%.

> TOWER DEFENSE GAME 🏰 Your castle is defended by five towers. Each tower has a 20% probability of disabling an invader before he reaches the gate. What are the chances of stopping him?

There's $0.2 + 0.2 + 0.2 + 0.2 + 0.2 = 1$, or a 100% chance of hitting the enemy, right? *Wrong!* Never sum the probabilities of independent events, that's a common mistake. Use complementary events twice:

- The 20% chance of hitting is complementary to the 80% chance of missing. The probability that all towers miss is: $0.8^5 \approx 0.33$.
- The event "all towers miss" is complementary to "at least one tower hits". The probability of stopping the enemy is: $1 - 0.33 = 0.67$.

The Gambler's Fallacy

If you flip a normal coin ten times, and you get ten heads, then on the 11th flip, are you more likely to get a tail? Or, by playing the lottery with the numbers 1 to 6, are you less likely to win than playing with more evenly spaced numbers?

Don't be a victim of the gambler's fallacy. Past events never affect the outcome of an independent event. Never. *Ever.* In a truly random lottery drawing, the chances of any specific numbers being chosen is the same as any other. There's no "hidden law" that forces numbers that weren't frequently chosen in the past to be chosen more often in the future.

Advanced Probabilities

There's far more to probability than we can cover here. Always remember to look for more tools when tackling complex problems. For example:

> TEAM BUILDING, AGAIN AND AGAIN 🐾 There are 23 candidates who want to join your team. For each candidate, you toss a coin and only hire if it shows heads. What are the chances of hiring seven people or less?

Yes, this is hard. Googling around will eventually lead you to the "binomial distribution". You can visualize this on Wolfram Alpha[14] by typing: `B(23,1/2) <= 7`.

---

[14]http://wolframalpha.com.

Conclusion

In this chapter, we've seen things that are intimately related to problem solving, but do not involve any actual coding. Section 1.1 explains why and how we should write things down. We create models for our problems, and use conceptual tools on the models we create. Section 1.2 provides a toolbox for handling logic, with boolean algebra and truth tables.

Section 1.3 shows the importance of counting possibilities and configurations of various problems. A quick back-of-the-envelope calculation can show you if a computation will be straightforward or fruitless. Novice programmers often lose time analyzing way too many scenarios. Finally, section 1.4 explains the basic rules of counting odds. Probability is very useful when developing solutions that must interact with our wonderful but uncertain world.

With this, we've outlined many important aspects of what academics call *Discrete Mathematics*. Many more fun theorems can be picked up from the references below or navigating Wikipedia. For instance, you can use the "Pigeonhole Principle" to prove at least two people in New York City have exactly the same number of hairs!

Some of what we learned here will be especially relevant in the next chapter, where we'll discover perhaps the most important aspect of computer science.

Reference

- Discrete Mathematics and its Applications, 7th Edition

    - Get it at https://code.energy/rosen

- Prof. Jeannette Wing's slides on computational thinking

    - Get it at https://code.energy/wing

CHAPTER 2

Complexity

> In almost every computation, a variety of arrangements
> for the processes is possible. It is essential to choose
> that arrangement which shall tend to minimize the
> time necessary for the calculation.
>
> —ADA LOVELACE

HOW MUCH TIME does it take to sort 26 shuffled cards? If instead you had 52 cards, would it take twice as long? How much longer would it take for a thousand decks of cards? The answer is intrinsic to the **method** used to sort the cards.

A method is a list of unambiguous instructions for achieving a goal. A method that always requires a finite series of operations is called an **algorithm**. For instance, a card-sorting algorithm is a method that will always specify some operations to sort a deck of 26 cards per suit and per rank.

Less operations need less computing power. We like fast solutions, so we monitor the number of operations in our algorithms. Many algorithms require a fast-growing number of operations when the input grows in size. For example, our card-sorting algorithm could take few operations to sort 26 cards, but four times as much operations to sort 52 cards!

To avoid bad surprises when our problem size grows, we find the algorithm's **time complexity**. In this chapter, you'll learn to:

- ⏱ Count and interpret **time** complexities,
- 📈 Express their growth with fancy **Big-O**'s,
- 🏃 Run away from **exponential** algorithms,
- 💾 Make sure you have enough computer **memory**.

But first, how do we define time complexity?

Time complexity is written $\mathbb{T}(n)$. It gives the number of operations the algorithm performs when processing an input of size n. We also refer to an algorithm's $\mathbb{T}(n)$ as its **running cost**. If our card-sorting algorithm follows $\mathbb{T}(n) = n^2$, we can predict how much longer it takes to sort a deck once we double its size: $\frac{\mathbb{T}(2n)}{\mathbb{T}(n)} = 4$.

Hope for the best, prepare for the worst

Isn't it faster to sort a pile of cards that's almost sorted already? Input size isn't the only characteristic that impacts the number of operations required by an algorithm. When an algorithm can have different values of $\mathbb{T}(n)$ for the same value of n, we resort to cases:

- BEST CASE: when the input requires the minimum number of operations for any input of that size. In sorting, it happens when the input is already sorted.
- WORST CASE: when the input requires the maximum number of operations for any input of that size. In many sorting algorithms, that's when the input was given in reverse order.
- AVERAGE CASE: refers to the average number of operations required for typical inputs of that size. For sorting, an input in random order is usually considered.

In general, the most important is the worst case. From there, you get a guaranteed baseline you can always count on. When nothing is said about the scenario, the worst case is assumed. Next, we'll see how to analyze a worst case scenario, hands on.

Figure 2.1 "Estimating Time", courtesy of http://xkcd.com.

2.1 Counting Time

We find the time complexity of an algorithm by counting the number of basic operations it requires for a hypothetical input of size n. We'll demonstrate it with **Selection Sort**, a sorting algorithm that uses a nested loop. An outer `for` loop updates the current position being sorted, and an inner `for` loop selects the item that goes in the current position:[1]

```
function selection_sort(list)
    for current ← 1 … list.length - 1
        smallest ← current
        for i ← current + 1 … list.length
            if list[i] < list[smallest]
                smallest ← i
        list.swap_items(current, smallest)
```

Let's see what happens with a list of n items, assuming the worst case. The outer loop runs $n - 1$ times and does two operations per run (one assignment and one swap) totaling $2n - 2$ operations. The inner loop first runs $n - 1$ times, then $n - 2$ times, $n - 3$ times, and so on. We know how to sum these types of sequences:[2]

$$\underset{\substack{\underbrace{}_{1^{\text{st}} \text{ pass of outer loop}}}}{\begin{array}{l}\text{\# of inner}\\\text{loop runs}\end{array} = n - 1} + \overbrace{\underset{2^{\text{nd}} \text{ pass of outer loop}}{\underbrace{n - 2}} + \cdots + 2 + 1}^{n-1 \text{ total runs of the outer loop.}}$$

$$= \sum_{i=1}^{n-1} i = \frac{(n-1)(n)}{2} = \frac{n^2 - n}{2}.$$

In the worst case, the `if` condition is always met. This means the inner loop does one comparison and one assignment $(n^2 - n)/2$ times, hence $n^2 - n$ operations. In total, the algorithm costs $2n - 2$ operations for the outer loop, plus $n^2 - n$ operations for the inner loop. We thus get the time complexity:

$$\mathbb{T}(n) = n^2 + n - 2.$$

---

[1]To understand a new algorithm, run it on paper with a small sample input.
[2]From sec. 1.3, $\sum_{i=1}^{n} i = n(n+1)/2$.

Now what? If our list size was $n = 8$ and we double it, the sorting time will be multiplied by:

$$\frac{\mathbb{T}(16)}{\mathbb{T}(8)} = \frac{16^2 + 16 - 2}{8^2 + 8 - 2} \approx 3.86.$$

If we double it again we will multiply time by 3.90. Double it over and over and find $3.94, 3.97, 3.98$. Notice how this gets closer and closer to 4? This means it would take four times as long to sort two million items than to sort one million items.

Understanding Growth

Say the input size of an algorithm is very large, and we increase it even more. To predict how the execution time will grow, we don't need to know all terms of $\mathbb{T}(n)$. We can approximate $\mathbb{T}(n)$ by its fastest-growing term, called the **dominant term**.

INDEX CARDS 📇 Yesterday, you knocked over one box of index cards. It took you two hours of Selection Sort to fix it. Today, you spilled ten boxes. How much time will you need to arrange the cards back in?

We've seen Selection Sort follows $\mathbb{T}(n) = n^2 + n - 2$. The fastest-growing term is n^2, therefore we can write $\mathbb{T}(n) \approx n^2$. Assuming there are n cards per box, we find:

$$\frac{\mathbb{T}(10n)}{\mathbb{T}(n)} \approx \frac{(10n)^2}{n^2} = 100.$$

It will take you approximately $100 \times (2\,\text{hours}) = 200\,\text{hours}$! What if we had used a different sorting method? For example, there's one called "Bubble Sort" whose time complexity is $\mathbb{T}(n) = 0.5n^2 + 0.5n$. The fastest-growing term then gives $\mathbb{T}(n) \approx 0.5n^2$, hence:

$$\frac{\mathbb{T}(10n)}{\mathbb{T}(n)} \approx \frac{0.5 \times (10n)^2}{0.5 \times n^2} = 100.$$

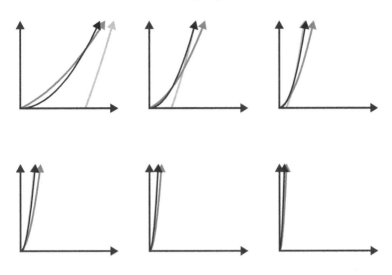

Figure 2.2 Zooming out n^2, $n^2 + n - 2$, and $0.5n^2 + 0.5n$, as n gets larger and larger.

The 0.5 coefficient cancels itself out! The idea that $n^2 + n - 2$ and $0.5n^2 + 0.5n$ both grow like n^2 isn't easy to get. How does the fastest-growing term of a function ignore all other numbers and dominate growth? Let's try to visually understand this.

In fig. 2.2, the two time complexities we've seen are compared to n^2 at different zoom levels. As we plot them for larger and larger values of n, their curves seem to get closer and closer. Actually, you can plug any numbers into the bullets of $\mathbb{T}(n) = \bullet \ n^2 + \bullet \ n + \bullet$, and it will still grow like n^2.

Remember, this effect of curves getting closer works if the fastest-growing term is the same. The plot of a function with a linear growth (n) never gets closer and closer to one with a quadratic growth (n^2), which in turn never gets closer and closer to one having a cubic growth (n^3).

That's why with very big inputs, algorithms with a quadratically growing cost perform a lot worse than algorithms with a linear cost. However they perform a lot better than those with a cubic cost. If you've understood this, the next section will be easy: we will just learn the fancy notation coders use to express this.

2.2   The Big-O Notation

There's a special notation to refer to classes of growth: the **Big-O notation**. A function with a fastest-growing term of 2^n *or weaker* is $\mathcal{O}(2^n)$; one with a quadratic *or weaker* growth is $\mathcal{O}(n^2)$; growing linearly *or less*, $\mathcal{O}(n)$, and so on. The notation is used for expressing the dominant term of algorithms' cost functions in the worst case—that's the standard way of expressing time complexity.[3]

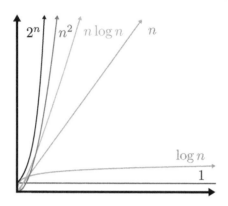

Figure 2.3   Different orders of growth often seen inside $\mathcal{O}$.

Both Selection Sort and Bubble Sort are $\mathcal{O}(n^2)$, but we'll soon discover $\mathcal{O}(n \log n)$ algorithms that do the same job. With our $\mathcal{O}(n^2)$ algorithms, $10\times$ the input size resulted in $100\times$ the running cost. Using a $\mathcal{O}(n \log n)$ algorithm, $10\times$ the input size results in only $10 \log 10 \approx 34\times$ the running cost.

When n is a million, n^2 is a trillion, whereas $n \log n$ is just a few million. Years running a quadratic algorithm on a large input could be equivalent to minutes if a $\mathcal{O}(n \log n)$ algorithm was used. That's why you need time complexity analysis when you design systems that handle very large inputs.

When designing a computational system, it's important to anticipate the most frequent operations. Then you can compare the Big-O costs of different algorithms that do these operations.[4] Also,

---

[3]We say 'oh', e.g., "that sorting algorithm is *oh-n-squared*".

[4]For the Big-O complexities of most algorithms that do common tasks, see http://code.energy/bigo.

most algorithms only work with specific input structures. If you choose your algorithms in advance, you can structure your input data accordingly.

Some algorithms always run for a constant duration regardless of input size—they're $\mathcal{O}(1)$. For example, checking if a number is odd or even: we see if its last digit is odd and *boom*, problem solved. No matter how big the number. We'll see more $\mathcal{O}(1)$ algorithms in the next chapters. They're amazing, but first let's see which algorithms are *not* amazing.

2.3 Exponentials

We say $\mathcal{O}(2^n)$ algorithms are **exponential time**. From the graph of growth orders (fig. 2.3), it doesn't seem the quadratic n^2 and the exponential 2^n are much different. Zooming out the graph, it's obvious the exponential growth brutally dominates the quadratic one:

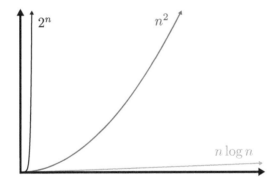

Figure 2.4 Different orders of growth, zoomed out. The linear and logarithmic curves grow so little they aren't visible anymore.

Exponential time grows *so much*, we consider these algorithms "not runnable". They run for very few input types, and require huge amounts of computing power if inputs aren't tiny. Optimizing every aspect of the code or using supercomputers doesn't help. The crushing exponential always dominates growth and keeps these algorithms unviable.

To illustrate the explosiveness of exponential growth, let's zoom out the graph even more and change the numbers (fig. 2.5). The exponential was reduced in power (from 2 to 1.5) and had its growth divided by a thousand. The polynomial had its exponent increased (from 2 to 3) and its growth multiplied by a thousand.

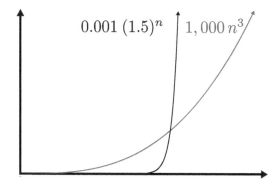

Figure 2.5 No exponential can be beaten by a polynomial. At this zoom level, even the $n \log n$ curve grows too little to be visible.

Some algorithms are even worse than exponential time algorithms. It's the case of **factorial time** algorithms, whose time complexities are $\mathcal{O}(n!)$. Exponential and factorial time algorithms are horrible, but we need them for the hardest computational problems: the famous **NP-complete** problems. We will see important examples of NP-complete problems in the next chapter. For now, remember this: the first person to find a non-exponential algorithm to a NP-complete problem gets a million dollars 💲[5] from the Clay Mathematics Institute.

It's important to recognize the class of problem you're dealing with. If it's known to be NP-complete, trying to find an optimal solution is fighting the impossible. Unless you're shooting for that million dollars.

---

[5]It has been proven a non-exponential algorithm for *any* NP-complete problem could be generalized to *all* NP-complete problems. Since we don't know if such an algorithm exists, you also get a million dollars if you prove an NP-complete problem cannot be solved by non-exponential algorithms!

2.4   Counting Memory

Even if we could perform operations infinitely fast, there would still be a limit to our computing power. During execution, algorithms need working storage to keep track of their ongoing calculations. This consumes **computer memory**, which is not infinite.

The measure for the working storage an algorithm needs is called **space complexity**. Space complexity analysis is similar to time complexity analysis. The difference is that we count computer memory, and not computing operations. We observe how space complexity evolves when the algorithm's input size grows, just as we do for time complexity.

For example, Selection Sort (sec. 2.1) just needs working storage for a fixed set of variables. The number of variables does not depend on the input size. Therefore, we say Selection Sort's space complexity is $\mathcal{O}(1)$: no matter what the input size, it requires the same amount of computer memory for working storage.

However, many other algorithms need working storage that grows with input size. Sometimes, it's impossible to meet an algorithm's memory requirements. You won't find an appropriate sorting algorithm with $\mathcal{O}(n \log n)$ time complexity *and* $\mathcal{O}(1)$ space complexity. Computer memory limitations sometimes force a trade-off. With low memory, you'll probably need an algorithm with slow $\mathcal{O}(n^2)$ time complexity because it has $\mathcal{O}(1)$ space complexity. In future chapters, we'll see how clever data handling can improve space complexity.

Conclusion

In this chapter, we learned algorithms can have different types of voracity for consuming computing time and computer memory. We've seen how to assess it with time and space complexity analysis. We learned to calculate time complexity by finding the *exact* $\mathbb{T}(n)$ function, the number of operations performed by an algorithm.

We've seen how to express time complexity using the Big-O notation ($\mathcal{O}$). Throughout this book, we'll perform simple time complexity analysis of algorithms using this notation. Many times, calculating $\mathbb{T}(n)$ is not necessary for inferring the Big-O complexity of an algorithm. We'll see easier ways to calculate complexity in the next chapter.

We've seen the cost of running exponential algorithms explode in a way that makes these algorithms not runnable for big inputs. And we learned how to answer these questions:

- Given different algorithms, do they have a significant difference in terms of operations required to run?
- Multiplying the input size by a constant, what happens with the time an algorithm takes to run?
- Would an algorithm perform a reasonable number of operations once the size of the input grows?
- If an algorithm is too slow for running on an input of a given size, would optimizing the algorithm, or using a supercomputer help?

In the next chapter, we'll focus on exploring how strategies underlying the design of algorithms are related to their time complexity.

Reference

- The Art of Computer Programming, Vol. 1, by Knuth

    – Get it at https://code.energy/knuth

- The Computational Complexity Zoo, by hackerdashery

    – Watch it at https://code.energy/pnp

- What is Big O, by Undefined Behavior

    – Watch it at https://code.energy/bigo-vid

CHAPTER 3

Strategy

> If you find a good move, look for a better one.
>
> —Emanuel Lasker

HISTORY REMEMBERS GENERALS who use sound strategy to achieve grand results. Excelling at problem solving requires being a good strategist. This chapter covers the main strategies for algorithm design. You will learn to:

- Handle repetitive tasks through **iteration**,
- Iterate elegantly using **recursion**,
- Use **brute force** when you're lazy but powerful,
- Test bad options and then **backtrack**,
- Save time with **heuristics** for a reasonable way out,
- **Divide and conquer** your toughest opponents,
- Identify old issues **dynamically** not to waste energy again,
- **Bound** your problem so the solution doesn't escape.

There are a lot of tools we will see here, but don't worry. We'll start with simple problems and progressively build better solutions as new techniques are uncovered. Soon enough, you will overcome your computational problems with sound and eloquent solutions.

3.1   Iteration

The iterative strategy consists in using loops (e.g. `for`, `while`) to repeat a process until a condition is met. Each step in a loop is called an **iteration**. It's great for running through an input and applying the same operations on every part of it. For example:

FISH REUNION 🐟 You're given a list of saltwater fish and a list of freshwater fish, both in alphabetical order. How do you create a list featuring all the fish in alphabetical order?

We can iteratively compare the top items of the two lists as follows:

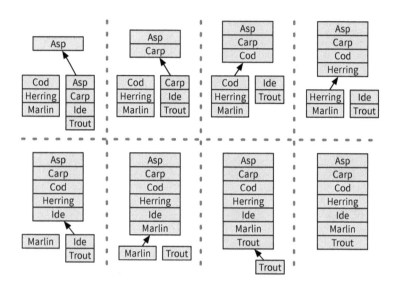

Figure 3.1 Merging two sorted lists into a third sorted list.

The process can be written in a single `while` loop:

```
function merge(sea, fresh)
    result ← List.new

    while not (sea.empty and fresh.empty)
        if sea.top_item > fresh.top_item
            fish ← sea.remove_top_item
        else
            fish ← fresh.remove_top_item
        result.append(fish)

    return result
```

It loops over all names in the inputs, performing a fixed number of operations for each name.[1] Hence the `merge` algorithm is $\mathcal{O}(n)$.

Nested Loops and the Power Set

In the previous chapter, we've seen how `selection_sort` uses a loop nested inside another one. Now we'll learn how to use a nested loop for computing **power sets**. Given a collection of objects S, the power set of S is the set containing all subsets of S.[2]

> EXPLORING SCENTS ✿ Floral fragrances are made combining scents from flowers. Given a set of flowers F, how do you list all fragrances that can be made?

Any fragrance is made from a subset of F, so its power set contains all possible fragrances. We can compute this power set iteratively. For zero flowers only one fragrance is possible: the one having *no scent*. For considering an additional flower, we duplicate the fragrances we already have, adding the new flower to the duplicated fragrances. It's easier to understand that visually:

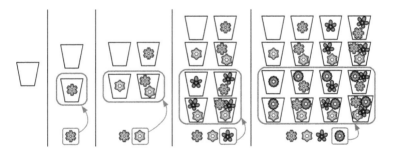

Figure 3.2   Iteratively listing all fragrances using four flowers.

The process can be described using loops. An outer loop keeps track of the next flower to consider. An inner loop duplicates the fragrances, adding the current flower to the duplicates.

---

[1]The input size is the number of items in both input lists combined. The `while` loop does three operations for each of these items, hence $\mathbb{T}(n) = 3n$.

[2]See Appendix III if you need a better explanation of sets.

```
function power_set(flowers)
    fragrances ← Set.new
    fragrances.add(Set.new)
    for each flower in flowers
        new_fragrances ← copy(fragrances)
        for each fragrance in new_fragrances
            fragrance.add(flower)
        fragrances ← fragrances + new_fragrances
    return fragrances
```

A single extra flower causes `fragrances` to double in size, indicating exponential growth ($2^{k+1} = 2 \times 2^k$). Algorithms that require double the operations if the input size increases by a single item are exponential, with $\mathcal{O}(2^n)$ time complexity.

Generating power sets is equivalent to generating truth tables (sec. 1.2). If we map each flower to a boolean variable, any fragrance is representable as `True`/`False` values of these variables. In these variables' truth table each row represents a possible fragrance formula.

3.2   Recursion

We say there's **recursion** when a function delegates work to *clones of itself*. A recursive algorithm will naturally come to mind for solving a problem defined in terms of *itself*. For example, take the famous Fibonacci sequence. It starts with two ones, and each subsequent number is the sum of the two previous numbers: $1, 1, 2, 3, 5, 8, 13, 21, \ldots$ How do you code a function that returns the nth Fibonnacci number?

```
function fib(n)
    if n ≤ 2
        return 1
    return fib(n - 1) + fib(n - 2)
```

Using recursion requires creativity for seeing how a problem can be stated in terms of itself. Checking if a word is palindrome[3] is

---

[3]Palindromes are read backwards like they read normally, e.g., *Ada, racecar*.

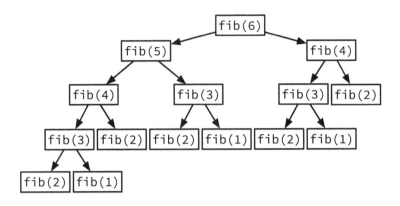

Figure 3.3 Calculating the 6th Fibonacci number recursively.

checking if the word changes if it's reversed. But also a word is palindrome if its first and last characters are equal and the sub-word between those characters is a palindrome:

```
function palindrome(word)
    if word.length ≤ 1
        return True
    if word.first_char ≠ word.last_char
        return False
    w ← word.remove_first_and_last_chars
    return palindrome(w)
```

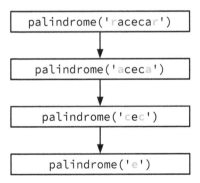

Figure 3.4 Checking if "racecar" is palindrome recursively.

Recursive algorithms have **base cases**, when the input is too small to be further reduced. Base cases for `fib` are numbers 1 and 2; for `palindrome`, they're words with one or zero characters.

Recursion vs. Iteration

Recursive algorithms are generally simpler and shorter than iterative ones. Compare this recursive algorithm with previous section's `power_set`, which doesn't use recursion:

```
function recursive_power_set(items)
    ps ← copy(items)
    for each e in items
        ps ← ps.remove(e)
        ps ← ps + recursive_power_set(ps)
        ps ← ps.add(e)
    return ps
```

This simplicity comes at a price. Recursive algorithms spawn numerous clones of themselves when they run, introducing a computational overhead. The computer must keep track of unfinished recursive calls and their partial calculations, requiring more memory. And extra CPU cycles are spent to switch from a recursive call to the next and back.

This potential problem can be visualized in **recursion trees**: a diagram showing how the algorithm spawns more calls as it delves deeper in calculations. We've seen recursion trees for calculating Fibonacci numbers (fig. 3.3) and checking palindrome words (fig. 3.4).

If performance must be maximized, we can avoid this overhead by rewriting recursive algorithms in a purely iterative form. Doing so is always possible. It's a trade: the iterative code generally runs faster but it's also more complex and harder to understand.

3.3   Brute Force

The brute force strategy solves problems by inspecting *all* of the problem's possible solution candidates. Also known as exhaustive search, this strategy is usually naive and unskilled: even when there are billions of candidates, it relies on the computer's sheer *force* for checking every single one.

Figure 3.5   Courtesy of http://geek-and-poke.com.

Let's see how we can use it to solve this problem:

> BEST TRADE 📈   You have the daily prices of gold for a interval of time. You want to find two days in this interval such that if you had bought then sold gold at those dates, you'd have made the maximum possible profit.

Buying at the lowest price and selling at the highest one isn't always possible: the lowest price could happen *after* the highest, and time travel isn't an option. A brute force approach finds the answer evaluating *all possible day pairs*. For each pair it finds the profit trading those days, comparing it to the best trade seen so far. We know the number of pairs of days in an interval increases quadratically as the interval increases.[4] Without writing the code, we're already sure it must be $\mathcal{O}(n^2)$.

Other strategies can be applied for solving the Best Trade problem with a better time complexity—we'll soon explore those. But in some cases, the brute force approach gives indeed the best possible time complexity. That's the case of the next problem:

KNAPSACK 🎒 You have a knapsack to carry products for selling. It holds up to a certain weight, not enough for carrying all your products—you must choose which ones to carry. Knowing the weight and sales value of each product, which choice of products gives the highest revenue?

The power set of your products[5] contains all possible product selections. A brute force approach simply checks all these selections. Since we already know how to compute power sets, the brute force algorithm is easy:

```
function knapsack(items, max_weight)
    best_value ← 0
    for each candidate in power_set(items)
        if total_weight(candidate) ≤ max_weight
            if sales_value(candidate) > best_value
                best_value ← sales_value(candidate)
                best_candidate ← candidate
    return best_candidate
```

For n products there are 2^n product selections. For each, we check if its total weight doesn't exceed the knapsack capacity and if its sales value is higher than best found so far. That's a fixed number of operations per product selection, meaning the algorithm is $\mathcal{O}(2^n)$.

However, not every product selection must be checked. Many leave the knapsack half empty, hinting there are better approaches.[6] Next we'll learn strategies to optimize our search for a solution, efficiently discarding as many solution candidates as possible.

---

[4] From sec. 1.3, there are $n(n+1)/2$ pairs of days in an interval of n days.

[5] Again, for an explanation of power sets, see Appendix III.

[6] The Knapsack problem is part of the **NP-complete** class we discussed in sec. 2.3. No matter the strategy, only exponential algorithms will solve it.

3.4 Backtracking

Have you ever played chess? Chess pieces move on an 8×8 board, attacking enemy pieces. The queen is the most powerful piece: it can attack pieces that occupy its row, its column, or its diagonals. The next strategy will be explained in the context of a famous chess problem:

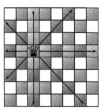

EIGHT QUEENS PUZZLE ♛ How do you place eight queens on the board such that no queens attack each other?

Try finding a solution manually: you'll see it's not trivial.[7] Figure 3.6 shows one of the ways queens can be peacefully positioned.

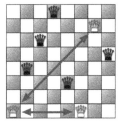 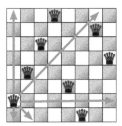

Figure 3.6 The leftmost queen attacks other queens. Moving her up, none of the queens attack each other.

We've seen in sec. 1.3 eight queens can be placed in the chessboard in over *four billion* ways. Solving this problem the brute force way inspecting all these possibilities is sloppy. Imagine the first two queens are placed on the board attacking each other: regardless where the next queens are placed, a solution isn't possible. Yet, a brute force approach would waste time with all these doomed queen placements.

Searching only *viable* queen placements is more efficient. The first queen can be placed anywhere. Viable placements for the next

---

[7]You can try it online: https://code.energy/8queens.

queens are limited by already placed queens: a queen cannot be placed in the attacking range of another queen. Placing queens following this rule, we're likely to get a board where it's impossible to place an additional queen before all eight queens are placed:

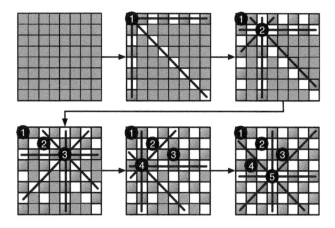

Figure 3.7   Placing a queen limits viable places for the next queens.

This can only mean the last queen was placed incorrectly. So we **backtrack**: we roll back the previous placement and continue the search. That's the essence of the backtracking strategy: keep on placing queens in valid positions. Once we get stuck, roll back the placement of the last queen and carry on. The process can be streamlined using recursion:

```
function queens(board)
    if board.has_8_queens
        return board
    for each position in board.unattacked_positions
        board.place_queen(position)
        solution ← queens(board)
        if solution
            return solution
        board.remove_queen(position)
    return False
```

If the board isn't already solved, it loops through all viable positions for the next queen. It uses recursion to check if placing a queen in each of these positions gives a solution. Here's how the process works:

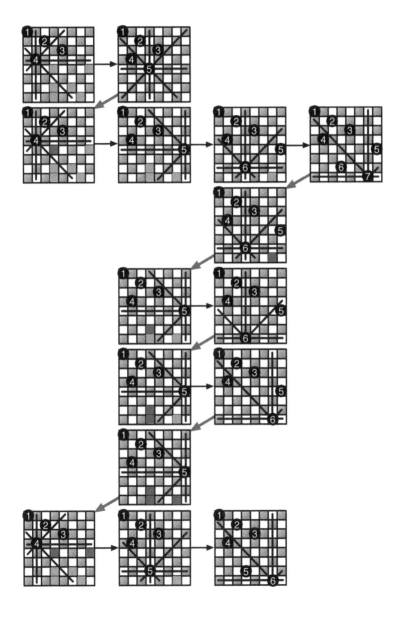

Figure 3.8 Backtracking in the 8 Queens Puzzle.

Backtracking works best in problems where the solution is a sequence of choices and making a choice restrains subsequent choices. It identifies as soon as possible the choices you've made cannot give you the solution you want, so you can sooner step back and try something else. *Fail early, fail often.*

3.5 Heuristics

In a standard chess game, you have 32 pieces of six types and 64 squares they can move on. After your first four moves, there are already 288 billion possible positions. Even the strongest players in the world can't find the best move. They rely on intuition to find one that is *good enough*. We can do the same with algorithms. A **heuristic method**, or simply a **heuristic**, is a method that leads to a solution without guaranteeing it is the best or optimal one. Heuristics can help when methods like brute force or backtracking are too slow. There are many funky heuristic approaches, but we'll focus on the simplest: *not* backtracking.

Greed

A very common heuristic approach to problems is the **greedy approach**. It consists in never coming back to previous choices. It's the opposite of backtracking. Try to make the best choice at each step, and don't question it later. Let's try this strategy to solve the Knapsack problem (sec. 3.3 👝), but with a twist:

> EVIL KNAPSACK 👹 A greedy burglar breaks into your home to steal the products you wanted to sell. He decides to use your knapsack to carry the stolen items. Which items will he steal? Remember, the less time he spends in your home, the less likely he is to get caught.

In essence, the optimal solution here should be the exact same as for the Knapsack problem. However, the burglar doesn't have time to calculate all packing combinations, nor does he have time to constantly backtrack and remove already packed items! A greedy packer will keep on putting the highest valued item in the knapsack until he can't fit more:

```
function greedy_knapsack(items, max_weight)
    bag_weight ← 0
    bag_items ← List.new
    for each item in sort_by_value(items)
        if max_weight ≥ bag_weight + item.weight
            bag_weight ← bag_weight + item.weight
            bag_items.append(item)
    return bag_items
```

We don't investigate how a choice affects future choices. This greedy approach finds a selection of items much faster than the brute force way. However, there's no guarantee it will find the selection with the highest possible combined value.

In computational thinking, greed is not only a sin of the evil. As an honest merchant, you may also want to pack the greedy way, or travel the greedy way:

> TRAVELING SALESMAN, AGAIN 🚐 A salesman must visit n given cities, ending the trip in the city he started. Which travel plan minimizes the total distance traveled?

As we've seen in sec. 1.3, the number of possible city permutations to consider explodes to a ridiculously high number even for few cities. It's extremely expensive (or impossible) to find the optimal solution for a Traveling Salesman problem with a few thousand cities.[8] But still, you need a route. Here's a simple greedy algorithm for this problem:

1. Visit the nearest unvisited city.
2. Repeat until all cities are visited.

Can you think of a better heuristic than a greedy approach? That's an active research question among computer scientists.

---

[8]The Traveling Salesman problem is in the NP-complete class we discussed in sec. 2.3. We can't find an optimal solution better than an exponential algorithm.

Figure 3.9 "Traveling Salesman Problem", from http://xkcd.com.

When Greed Trumps Power

Choosing a heuristic over a classic algorithm is a trade-off. How far from the optimal knapsack or travel route are you willing to settle for? Make the choice case by case.

However, don't ignore heuristics altogether when you absolutely require the optimal solution. A heuristic approach to a problem can sometimes lead to the best solution. For example, you might develop a greedy algorithm that systematically finds the same solution as would a powerful brute force attack. Let's see how this can happen:

> POWER GRID ⚡ Settlements in a remote area got no electricity, but one of the settlements is building a power plant. Electricity can be distributed from a settlement to the next linking them via power lines. How do you link all settlements into a power grid using the least wire?

This problem can be solved simply:

1. From settlements having no power, pick the one which is closest to a settlement that has power, and link those two.
2. Repeat until all settlements are powered.

At each step we choose a pair of settlements to connect, considering what looks best at the current moment. Even though we don't inves-

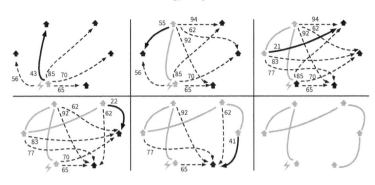

Figure 3.10 Solving the Power Grid problem with greedy choices.

tigate how a choice affects future choices, connecting the nearest non-powered settlement is always the right choice. We were lucky here: the structure of this problem was perfectly suited to be solved by a greedy algorithm. In the next section, we'll see problem structures that are suited to a great general's strategy.

3.6 Divide and Conquer

Once an enemy is divided in smaller problems, it's easier to conquer. Caesar and Napoleon ruled Europe by dividing and conquering their enemies. You can crack problems using the same strategy, especially those with **optimal substructure**. Problems with optimal substructure can be divided into similar but smaller subproblems. They can be divided over and over until subproblems become easy. Then subproblem solutions are combined for obtaining the original problem's solution.

Divide and Sort

If we have a big list to sort, we can split it into halves: each half-list becomes a sorting subproblem. To sort the big list, subproblem solutions (i.e., the sorted halves) can be merged in a single list using the `merge` algorithm.[9] But how will we sort our two subproblems? They are themselves split into *sub*subproblems, sorted and merged.

---

[9]The first algorithm we've seen in this chapter (sec. 3.1).

The new *sub*subproblems will also be split, sorted, and merged. The splitting continues until we hit the base case: a one-item list. A one-item list is already sorted!

```
function merge_sort(list)
    if list.length = 1
        return list
    left ← list.first_half
    right ← list.last_half
    return merge(merge_sort(left),
                 merge_sort(right))
```

This elegant recursive algorithm is called **Merge Sort**. As for the Fibonacci sequence (sec. 3.2), a recursion tree helps to see how many times the `merge_sort` function calls itself:

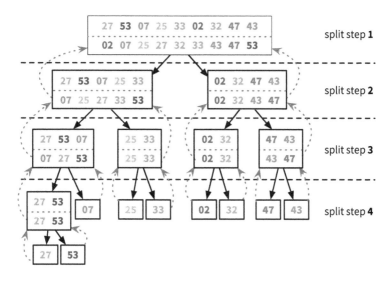

Figure 3.11 Sample Merge Sort execution. Rectangles are individual `merge_sort` calls, with inputs on top and outputs at the bottom.

Let's now find Merge Sort's time complexity. To do this, we're first going to count the operations generated by each individual split step. Then, we'll count how many split steps there are in total.

COUNTING OPERATIONS Say we have a big list of size n. When called, the `merge_sort` function performs the following operations:

- Splits list in halves, which does not depend on list size: $\mathcal{O}(1)$,
- A `merge`: we recall from sec. 3.1 that `merge` is $\mathcal{O}(n)$,
- Two `merge_sort` recursive calls that are *not* counted.[10]

Since we keep the strongest term and don't count recursive calls, the time complexity of the function is $\mathcal{O}(n)$. Let's now count the time complexity of each split step:

Split step 1. The `merge_sort` function is called for a list of n items. The time complexity of this step is $\mathcal{O}(n)$.

Split step 2. The `merge_sort` function is called twice, each time for $n/2$ items. We find $2 \times \mathcal{O}(n/2) = \mathcal{O}(n)$.

Split step 3. The `merge_sort` function is called four times, each time for $n/4$ items: $4 \times \mathcal{O}(n/4) = \mathcal{O}(n)$.

$$\vdots$$

Split step x. The `merge_sort` function is called 2^x times, each for a list of $n/2^x$ items: $2^x \times \mathcal{O}(n/2^x) = \mathcal{O}(n)$.

The split steps all have the same complexity of $\mathcal{O}(n)$. Merge Sort's time complexity is thus $x \times \mathcal{O}(n)$, where x is the number of split steps necessary for its full execution.[11]

COUNTING STEPS How do we evaluate x? We know recursive functions stop to call themselves once they hit their base case. Our base case is a one-item list. We've also seen that split step x works on lists of $n/2^x$ items. Therefore:

$$\frac{n}{2^x} = 1 \quad \rightarrow \quad 2^x = n \quad \rightarrow \quad x = \log_2 n.$$

If you're not familiar with the $\log_2$ function, don't be scared! $x = \log_2 n$ is just another way to write $2^x = n$. Coders love log growth.

---

[10]Operations performed by recursive calls are counted in the next split step!

[11]We can't ignore x because it's not a constant. If the list size n doubles, you'll need one more split step. If n quadruples, you'll need two more split steps.

See how slowly the number of required split steps increases[12] with the total number of items to sort:

Table 3.1 Number of split steps required for inputs of different sizes.

Input size (n)	$\log_2 n$	Split steps required
10	3.32	4
100	6.64	7
1,024	10.00	10
1,000,000	19.93	20
1,000,000,000	29.89	30

Merge Sort's time complexity is thus $\log_2 n \times \mathcal{O}(n) = \mathcal{O}(n \log n)$. That's a *huge* improvement over the $\mathcal{O}(n^2)$ Selection Sort. Do you remember the performance gap between log-linear and quadratic algorithms we've seen last chapter in fig. 2.4? Even if a faster computer crunches the $\mathcal{O}(n^2)$ algorithm, it will end up slower than a computer crunching the $\mathcal{O}(n \log n)$ algorithm:

Table 3.2 For big inputs, $\mathcal{O}(n \log n)$ algorithms in slow computers are *much* faster than $\mathcal{O}(n^2)$ algorithms in 1000× faster computers.

Input Size	Quadratic	Log-linear
196 (countries in the world)	38 ms	2 s
44K (airports in the world)	32 min	12 min
171K (English dictionary words)	8 hours	51 min
1M (inhabitants of Hawaii)	12 days	6 hours
19M (inhabitants of Florida)	11 years	6 days
130M (books ever published)	500 years	41 days
4.7G (web pages of the Internet)	700K years	5 years

See for yourself: write a log-linear and a quadratic sorting algorithm, compare how they perform for sorting random lists of different sizes. For big inputs, such complexity improvements are often vital. Let's now divide and conquer the problems we had tried brute force on.

---

[12]Any process that reduces an input step-by-step, dividing it by a constant factor in each step, takes a logarithmic number of steps to fully reduce the input.

Divide and Trade

Divide and conquer is a better approach for the Best Trade problem (sec. 3.3 ⚑) than simple brute force. Splitting the price history in half leads to two subproblems: finding the best trade in the former half and in the latter half. The best trade in the full period is either:

1. The best trade that buys and sells in the first half.
2. The best trade that buys and sells in the second half.
3. The best trade buying in the first half, selling in the second.

The first two cases are the solutions of the subproblems. The third case is easy to find: buy at the lowest price of the first half and sell at the highest price of the second half. For inputs over just one day, the only possible trade is buying and selling the same day, yielding a profit of zero.

```
function trade(prices)
    if prices.length = 1
        return 0
    former ← prices.first_half
    latter ← prices.last_half
    case3 ← max(latter) - min(former)
    return max(trade(former), trade(latter), case3)
```

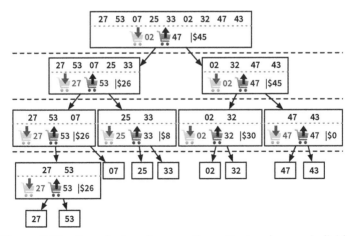

Figure 3.12 Sample `trade` execution. Rectangles are individual `trade` calls with their input and output.

When `trade` is called it performs trivial comparison and split operations and finds the maximum and minimum on halves of the input. Finding the maximum or minimum of n items requires inspecting each of the n items, so an isolated `trade` call costs $\mathcal{O}(n)$.

You'll notice `trade`'s recursion tree (fig. 3.12) is very similar to that of Merge Sort (fig. 3.11). It also has $\log_2 n$ split steps, where each split step costs $\mathcal{O}(n)$. Therefore, `trade` is also $O(n \log n)$—a huge improvement over the previous $\mathcal{O}(n^2)$ brute force approach.

Divide and Pack

The Knapsack problem (sec. 3.3 🎒) can also be divided and conquered. Remember, we have n products to choose from. We will enumerate each item property as follows:

- w_i is the ith item's weight,
- v_i is the ith item's value.

An item's index i can be any number between 1 and n. The maximum revenue for a knapsack of capacity c choosing among the n items is $K(n, c)$. If an extra item $i = n + 1$ is considered, it may or may not improve the maximum possible revenue, which becomes the highest of:

1. $K(n, \ c)$, if the extra item is not selected.
2. $K(n, \ c - w_{n+1}) + v_{n+1}$, if the extra item is selected.

Case 1 disregards the new item. Case 2 includes the new item, and selects among the original items ensuring there's enough space for it. This means we can define the solution for n items as the maximum of subsolutions for $n - 1$ items:

$$K(n, c) = \max(\ K(n - 1, \ c),$$
$$K(n - 1, \ c - w_n) + v_n \ ).$$

By now it should be easy to transform this recursive formula into a recursive algorithm. Figure 3.13 illustrates how the recursive process solves a sample problem. Rectangles that appear more than once were highlighted, as they represent identical subproblems that are being computed more than once in the process. Next we'll learn how to gain performance by avoiding such repeated computations.

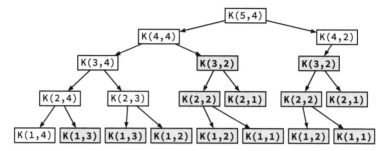

Figure 3.13 Solving a Knapsack problem with 5 items and knapsack capacity 4. Items numbered 5 and 4 weight two, the others weight one.

3.7 Dynamic Programming

Sometimes identical computations are performed multiple times when solving a problem.[13] **Dynamic programming** is identifying repeated subproblems in order to compute them only once. One common way to do this is a method similar to memorizing, with similar spelling. 🤓

Memoizing Fibonacci

Remember the algorithm to calculate Fibonacci numbers? Its recursion tree (fig. 3.3) shows `fib(3)` being calculated multiple times. We can fix it by storing `fib` calculations as we do them, only spawning `fib` calls for calculations not already stored. This trick for reusing partial calculations is called **memoization**. It gives `fib` a performance boost:

```
M[1] ← 1
M[2] ← 2
function dfib(n)
    if n not in M
        M[n] ← dfib(n-1) + dfib(n-2)
    return M[n]
```

---

[13]Problems where this happen are said to have **overlapping subproblems**.

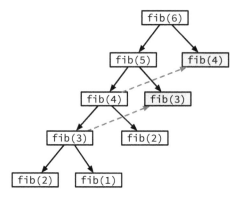

Figure 3.14 Recursion tree for dfib. Green rectangles represent calls which are not recalculated.

Memoizing Knapsacks

It's obvious there are multiple repeated calls in the Knapsack's recursion tree (fig. 3.13). Using the same technique that was used in the Fibonacci function these recalculations are avoided, resulting in less computation.

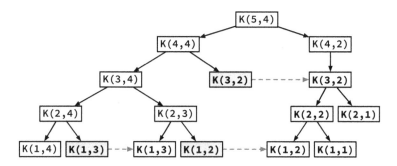

Figure 3.15 Solving the Knapsack recursively with memoization.

Dynamic programming can turn super slow code into reasonably paced code. Carefully analyze your algorithms to ensure they're free of repeated computations. As we'll see next, sometimes finding overlapping subproblems can be tricky.

Bottom-up Best Trade

The recursion tree for `trade` (fig. 3.12) has no repeated calls, yet it's doing repeated computations. It scans the input to find maximum and minimum values. Afterwards the input is split in half, and recursive calls scan the input again to find maxima and minima in those halves.[14] We need a different approach for avoiding these repeated scans.

So far we resorted to a **top-down** approach, where inputs are reduced until base cases are reached. But we can also go **bottom-up**: calculate base cases first, and assemble them over and over again until we get the general solution. Let's solve the Best Trade problem (sec. 3.3 ▪) that way.

Let's call $P(n)$ the price on the nth day. Let's call $B(n)$ the best day to buy if we're selling on the nth day. If we sell on the first day, we can only buy on day 1, therefore $B(1) = 1$. But if we sell on the second day, $B(2)$ can be either equal to 1 or 2:

- $P(2) < P(1) \rightarrow B(2) = 2$ (buy and sell on day 2).
- $P(2) \geq P(1) \rightarrow B(2) = 1$ (buy on day 1, sell on day 2).

The day with the lowest price *before* day 3 but *not on* day 3 is $B(2)$. So for $B(3)$,

- $P(3) <$ price on day $B(2) \rightarrow B(3) = 3$.
- $P(3) \geq$ price on day $B(2) \rightarrow B(3) = B(2)$.

Notice the day with the lowest price *before* day 4 is $B(3)$. In fact, for every n, $B(n-1)$ is the day with the lowest price before day n. Using this we can express $B(n)$ in terms of $B(n-1)$:

$$B(n) = \begin{cases} n & \text{if } P(n) < P(B(n-1)), \\ B(n-1) & \text{otherwise.} \end{cases}$$

---

[14]You need to find the tallest man, the tallest woman and the tallest person in a room. Would you measure everybody for finding the tallest person, then measure every woman and every man for the tallest man and woman?

Having all pairs $[n, B(n)]$ for each day n in the input, the solution is the pair giving the highest profit. This algorithm solves the problem by calculating all B values bottom-up:

```
function trade_dp(P)
    B[1] ← 1
    sell_day ← 1
    best_profit ← 0

    for each n from 2 to P.length
        if P[n] < P[B[n-1]]
            B[n] ← n
        else
            B[n] ← B[n-1]

        profit ← P[n] - P[B[n]]
        if profit > best_profit
            sell_day ← n
            best_profit ← profit

    return (sell_day, B[sell_day])
```

This algorithm performs a fixed set of simple operations per item in the input list, therefore, it's $\mathcal{O}(n)$. That's a huge performance leap from the previous $\mathcal{O}(n \log n)$ algorithm—and downright incomparable to the $\mathcal{O}(n^2)$ brute force approach. It's also $\mathcal{O}(n)$ in space, since the auxiliary vector B has as many items as the input. In Appendix IV, you can see how to gain computer memory by making the algorithm $\mathcal{O}(1)$ in space.

3.8   Branch and Bound

Many problems involve minimizing or maximizing a target value: find the shortest path, get the maximum profit, etc. They're called **optimization problems**. When the solution is a sequence of choices, we often use a strategy called **branch and bound**. Its aim is to gain time by quickly detecting and discarding bad choices. To understand how bad choices are detected, we first need to learn the concepts of upper and lower bounds.

Upper and Lower Bounds

Bounds refer to the range of a value. An **upper bound** sets a limit on how high the value can be. A **lower bound** is the least one can hope for: it guarantees the value is equal to it or greater.

We can often easily get suboptimal solutions: a short path, but maybe not the shortest; a big profit, but maybe not the biggest. These solutions provide bounds to the optimal solution. For instance, the shortest route between two places is never shorter than their straight linear distance. The linear distance is thus a lower bound of the shortest driving distance.

In the Evil Knapsack problem (sec. 3.5 ☠) the profit given by `greedy_knapsack` is a lower bound to the optimal profit (it may or may not be close to the optimal profit). Now imagine a version of the Knapsack problem in which items are all made of powder, so we can put fractions of items in the knapsack. This version of the problem can be solved in a simple greedy way: keep packing items with the highest value/weight ratio:

```
function powdered_knapsack(items, max_weight)
    bag_weight ← 0
    bag_items ← List.new
    items ← sort_by_value_weight_ratio(items)
    for each i in items
        weight ← min(max_weight - bag_weight,
                        i.weight)
        bag_weight ← bag_weight + weight
        value ← weight * i.value_weight_ratio
        bagged_value ← bagged_value + value
        bag_items.append(item, weight)
    return bag_items, bag_value
```

Adding the restriction that items are indivisible can only make the highest possible profit decrease because we'll have to replace the last added item with something worth less. This means `powdered_knapsack` gives an upper bound of the optimal profit with indivisible items.[15]

---

[15]The technique of removing restrictions from problems is called **relaxation**. It's often used for computing bounds in optimization problems.

Branch and Bound in the Knapsack Problem

We've seen finding the optimal profit in a Knapsack problem requires an expensive $\mathcal{O}(2^n)$ computation. However, we can quickly get upper and lower bounds on the optimal profit using powdered_knapsack and greedy_knapsack. Let's try this on a sample Knapsack problem:

Product	Value	Weight	Value/Weight Ratio	Max Capacity
A	2	2	1.00	
B	15	7	2.14	
C	16	3	5.33	10
D	12	2	6.00	
E	8	2	4.00	
F	3	4	0.75	

The figure to the right illustrates the situation before we start packing. The first box shows unpacked items to consider. The second box shows the knapsack's available capacity and which items it contains. 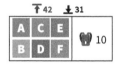 Running greedy_knapsack gives a profit of 31, and powdered_knapsack gives a profit 42.43. That means the optimum profit is somewhere between 31 and 42. Section 3.6 taught us this problem with n items can be divided into two subproblems with $n - 1$ items. The first subproblem will consider the item A is taken, the other will consider it's *not* taken:

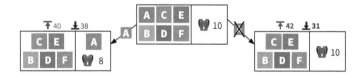

We calculate upper and lower bounds on the two subproblems. One has a lower bound of 38: now we know the optimal solution is between 38 and 42. Let's explore the subproblem on the right, as it has more interesting bounds:

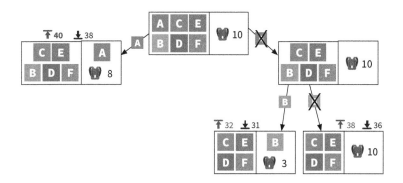

Now the leftmost subproblem became the one having the most promising upper bound. Let's continue our exploration splitting that subproblem:

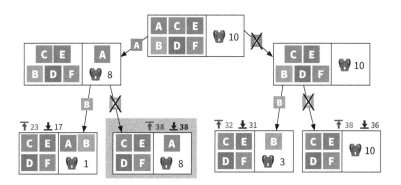

Now we can draw important conclusions. The highlighted subproblem has a lower bound of 38, which is equal to its upper bound. That means the optimal profit from this subproblem must be *exactly* 38. Furthermore, notice 38 is bigger than the upper bounds on all the other branches of subproblems pending exploration. No other subproblem branch can give a better profit than 38, meaning we can remove these branches from our search.

The wise use of upper and lower bounds allowed us to find the optimal profit with minimal computational effort. We dynamically adapted our search space as we were exploring possibilities. To recap, here's how branch and bound works:

1. Divide the problem into subproblems,
2. Find upper and lower bounds of each new subproblem,
3. Compare subproblem bounds of all branches,
4. Return to step 1 with the most promising subproblem.

You might remember the backtracking strategy (sec. 3.4) also led to the solution without exploring every possible solution candidate. In backtracking, we remove paths after having explored them as far as we can, and we stop when we're OK with a solution. With branch and bound, we predict which paths are worst and we avoid wasting energy exploring them.

Conclusion

Solving problems is navigating their space of possible solutions to find the correct one. We learned several ways to do it. The simplest is brute force: checking every item in the search space one by one.

We've seen how to systematically divide problems into smaller ones, reaping big performance gains. Dividing problems repeatedly often involves dealing with the same subproblems. In these cases it's important to use dynamic programming to avoid repeating the same computations.

We saw how backtracking can optimize some types of brute force searches. For problems where upper or lower bounds can be estimated, we've seen how to use that for finding solutions faster via branch and bound. And heuristics are used when the cost to calculate the optimum solution isn't acceptable.

All these strategies we've seen are for operating with data. Next we'll learn the most common ways data is organized in the computer's memory, and how that affects the performance of the most common data operations.

Reference

- Algorithm Design, 1st Edition, by Kleinberg

  – Get it at https://code.energy/kleinberg

- Choosing Algorithm Design Strategy, by Shailendra Nigam

  – Get it at https://code.energy/nigam

- Dynamic programming, by Umesh V. Vazirani

  – Get it at https://code.energy/vazirani

Chapter 4

Data

> Good programmers worry about data
> structures and their relationships.
>
> — Linus Torvalds

C ONTROL OVER DATA is essential to computer science: computational processes are made of data operations that transform input into output. But algorithms usually don't specify *how* their data operations are performed. For instance, `merge` (sec. 3.1) relies on unspecified external code to create lists of numbers, to check if lists are empty, and to append items into lists. The `queens` algorithm (sec. 3.4) does the same: it doesn't care how operations on the chessboard are made, nor how positions are stored in memory. These details are hidden behind what we call **abstractions**. In this chapter, we'll learn:

- ✦ How **abstract data types** keep your code clean,
- ✗ **Common abstractions** you need in your toolbox,
- ▦ Different ways to **structure data** in memory.

But before we dive into all this, let's first understand what the terms "abstraction" and "data type" mean.

Abstractions

Abstractions let us omit details; they are an interface for reaping the functionality of complex things in a simple way. For instance, cars hide complex mechanics beneath a driving panel, such that anyone can easily learn to drive without understanding any engineering.

In software, **procedural abstractions** hide complexities of a process beneath a procedure call. In the `trade` algorithm (sec. 3.6), the `min` and `max` procedures hide *how* the minimum and maximum numbers are found, making the algorithm simpler. With abstractions on top of other abstractions, we can build modules[1] that allow us to do complex stuff with single procedures, like this:

```
html ← fetch_source("https://code.energy")
```

In one line of code, we fetched a website's source code, even though the inner workings of that task are extremely complex.[2]

Data abstractions will be a central topic in this chapter. They hide details of data-handling processes. But before we can understand how data abstraction works, we need to solidify our understanding of data types.

Data Type

We distinguish different types of fasteners (like screws, bolts, and nails) according to the operations we can perform on them (like screwing, wrenching, and hammering). Similarly, we distinguish different **types of data** according to the operations that can be performed on the data.

For instance, a data variable that can be split in positional characters, that can be converted to upper or lower case, that can receive appended characters, is of the String type. Strings represent texts. A data variable that can be inverted, that can receive XOR, OR, AND operations, is of the Boolean type. Booleans can be either `True` or `False`. Variables that can be summed, divided, subtracted, are of the Number type.

Every data type is associated with a specific set of procedures. The procedures that work on variables that store Lists are different to the ones that work on variables that store Sets, which are different from the ones that work on Numbers.

---

[1]A **module**, or **library**, is a piece of software that provides generic computational procedures. They can be included on demand in other pieces of software.

[2]It involves resolving a domain name, creating a TCP network socket, doing SSL encryption handshakes, and much more.

4.1 Abstract Data Types

An **Abstract Data Type** (ADT) is the specification of a group of operations that make sense for a given data type. They define an interface for working with variables holding data of a given type—hiding all details of how data is stored and operated in memory.

When our algorithms needs to operate on data, we don't directly instruct the computer's memory to read and write. We use external data-handling modules that provide procedures defined in ADTs.

For example, to operate with variables that store lists, we need: procedures for creating and deleting lists; procedures for accessing or removing the nth item of a list; and a procedure for appending a new item to a list. The definitions of these procedures (their names and what they do) are a List ADT. We can work with lists by exclusively relying on these procedures. That way, we never manipulate the computer's memory directly.

Advantages of Using ADTs

SIMPLICITY ADTs make our code simpler to understand and modify. By omitting details from data handling procedures, you focus on the big picture: the problem-solving process of the algorithm.

FLEXIBILITY There are different ways to structure data in memory, leading to different data-handling modules for a same data type. We should choose the best for the situation at hand. Modules implementing the same ADT provide the same procedures. This means we can change the way the data is stored and manipulated *just* by using a different data-handling module. It's like cars: electric cars and gas-powered cars all have the same driving interface. Anyone who can drive a car can effortlessly switch to any other.

REUSABILITY We can use the same data-handling modules in projects that require handling data of the same type. For instance, both `power_set` and `recursive_power_set` from last chapter operate with variables representing sets. This means we can use the same `Set` module in both algorithms.

ORGANIZATION We usually need to operate several data types: numbers, text, geographical coordinates, images, and more. To better organize our code, we create distinct modules that each host code specific to a data type. That's called **separation of concerns**: parts of code that deal with the same logical aspect should be grouped in their own, separate module. When they're entangled with other functionalities, we call it *spaghetti code*.

CONVENIENCE We can get a data-handling module coded by someone else, and learn to use the procedures defined by its ADT. Then we can use these procedures to operate with variables of a new data type right away. Understanding how the data-handling module works isn't required.

BUG-FIXING If you're using a bug-free data-handling module, your code will be free of data-handling bugs. If you find a bug in a data-handling module, fixing it once means you instantly fix all parts of your code affected by the bug.

4.2 Common Abstractions

To solve a computational problem, it is very important to understand the type of data you're working on and the operations you'll need to perform on it. Deciding the ADT you'll use is equally important. Next, we present well known Abstract Data Types you should be familiar with. They appear in countless algorithms. They even come built-in with many programming languages.

Primitive Data Types

Primitive data types are those with built-in support in the programming language you're using—they work without external modules. These always include integers, floating points,[3] and generic operations with them (addition, subtraction, division). Most languages also come with built-in support for storing text, booleans and other simple data types in their variables.

---

[3]Floating points are a common way to represent numbers that have a decimal.

The Stack

Picture a pile of papers. You can put a sheet onto the top of the pile, or take the top sheet off. The first sheet to be added is always the last to be removed. The **Stack** is used when we have a pile of items, and only work with its top item. The item on top is *always* the pile's most recently inserted one. A Stack implementation must provide at least these two operations:

- **push(e)**: add an item e to the top of the stack,
- **pop()**: retrieve and remove the item on top of the stack.

More "advanced" stacks may provide more operations: to check whether the stack is empty, or to get the number of items currently in the stack.

Processing data this way is know as **LIFO** (Last-In, First-Out); we only ever remove items from the top, which always has the stack's most recent insertion. The Stack is an important data type that occurs in many algorithms. For implementing the "undo" feature in your text editor, every edition you make is pushed onto a stack. Should you want to undo, the text editor pops an edition from the stack and reverts it.

To implement backtracking (sec. 3.4) without recursive algorithms, you must remember the sequence of choices that got you to the current spot in a stack. When exploring a new node, we push a reference to the node into a stack. To go back, simply **pop()** from the stack to get a reference of where to go back to.

The Queue

The **Queue** is the Stack's antagonist. It's also used for storing and retrieving items, but the retrieved item is always the one in *front* of the Queue, i.e., the one that has been on the queue the longest. Don't be confused, that's just like a real-life queue of people waiting in a restaurant! The Queue's essential operations are:

- **enqueue(e)**: add an item e to the back of the queue,
- **dequeue()**: remove the item at the front of the queue.

The Queue works by organizing data the **FIFO** way (First-In, First-Out), because the first (and oldest) item that was inserted in the queue is always the first to leave the queue.

Queues are used in many computing scenarios. If you are implementing an online pizza service, you will likely store the pizza orders in a queue. As a thought exercise, think about what would be different if your pizza restaurant was designed to serve the orders using a Stack instead of a Queue. 👻

The Priority Queue

The **Priority Queue** is similar to the Queue, with the difference that enqueued items must have an assigned *priority*. People waiting for medical attention in a hospital is a real life example of a Priority Queue. The urgent cases receive top priority and go directly to the front of the queue, whereas the minor cases are added to the bottom of the queue. These are the Priority Queue's operations:

- **enqueue(e, p)**: add an item **e** to the queue according to the priority level **p**,
- **dequeue()**: remove the item at the front of the queue and return it.

In a computer there are typically many running processes but only one (or a few) CPUs to execute them. An operating system organizes all these processes waiting for execution in a Priority Queue. Each process waiting in the queue is assigned a priority level. The operating system dequeues a process and lets it run for a little while. Afterwards, if the process isn't finished it gets enqueued again. The operating system keeps repeating this.

Some processes are more time-sensitive and get immediate CPU time, others wait in the queue longer. The process that gets input from the keyboard typically receives a super-high priority. If the keyboard stops responding, the user might believe the computer crashed and try to cold-restart it, which is *never* good.

The List

When storing a bunch of items, you sometimes need more flexibility. For instance, you could want to freely reorder the items; or to access, insert and remove items at any position. In these cases, the **List** is handy. Commonly defined operations in a List ADT include:

- **insert(n, e)**: insert the item e at position n,
- **remove(n)**: remove the item at position n,
- **get(n)**: get the item at position n,
- **sort()**: sort the items in the list,
- **slice(start, end)**: return a sub-list slice starting at the position start up until the position end,
- **reverse()**: reverse the order of the list.

The List is one of the most used ADTs. For instance, if you need to store links to the most frequently accessed files in a system, a list is ideal: you can sort the links for display purposes, and remove links at will as the corresponding files become less frequently accessed.

The Stack or Queue should be preferred when the flexibility of List isn't needed. Using a simpler ADT ensures data is handled in a strict and robust way (FIFO or LIFO). It also makes the code easier to understand: knowing a variable is a Stack helps to see how data flows in and out.

The Sorted List

The **Sorted List** is useful when you need to maintain an *always sorted* list of items. In these cases, instead of figuring out the right position before each insertion in the list (and manually sorting it periodically), we use a Sorted List. Its insertions always keep the list sorted. None of its operations allow reordering its items: the list is guaranteed to be always sorted. The Sorted List has fewer operators than the List:

- **insert(e)**: insert item e at the right position in the list,
- **remove(n)**: remove the item at the position n in the list,
- **get(n)**: get the item at position n.

The Map

The **Map** (aka **Dictionary**) is used to store mappings between two objects: a **key** object and a **value** object. You can query a map with a key and get its associated value. For instance, you might use a map to store a user's ID number as key, and its full name as value. Then, given the ID number of a user, the map returns the related name. The operations for the Map are:

- **set(key, value)**: add a key-value mapping,
- **delete(key)**: remove key and its associated value,
- **get(key)**: retrieve the value that was associated to key.

The Set

The **Set** represents unordered groups of *unique* items, like mathematical sets described in Appendix III. They're used when the order of items you need to store is meaningless, or if you must ensure no items in the group occurs more than once. The common Set operations are:

- **add(e)**: add an item to the set or produce an error if the item is already in the set,
- **list()**: list the items in the set,
- **delete(e)**: remove an item from the set.

With these ADTs, you as a coder learned to interact with data, like a driver uses a car's dashboard. Now let's try to understand how the wires are structured *behind* that dashboard.

4.3   Structures

An Abstract Data Type only describes how variables of a given data type are operated. It provides a list of operations, but doesn't explain *how* data operations happen. Conversely, **data structures** describe *how* data is to be organized and accessed in the computer's memory. They provide ways for implementing ADTs in data-handling modules.

There are different ways to implement ADTs because there are different data structures. Selecting an ADT implementation that uses the best data structure according to your needs is essential for creating efficient computer programs. Next we'll explore the most common data structures and learn their strengths and weaknesses.

The Array

The **Array** is the simplest way to store a bunch of items in computer memory. It consists in allocating a sequential space in the computer memory, and writing your items sequentially in that space, marking the end of the sequence with a special NULL token.

Each object in an array occupies the same amount of space in memory. Imagine an array starting at memory address s, where each item occupy b bytes. The nth item in the array can be obtained fetching b bytes starting from memory position $s + (b \times n)$.

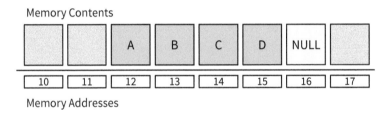

Memory Contents

		A	B	C	D	NULL	
10	11	12	13	14	15	16	17

Memory Addresses

Figure 4.1 An array in the computer's memory.

This lets us access any item from an array *instantly*. The Array is especially useful for implementing the Stack, but can also used to implement Lists and Queues. Arrays are simple to code and have the advantage of instant access time. But they also have disadvantages.

It can be impractical to allocate large amounts of sequential space in the memory. If you need to grow an array, there might not be enough free space adjacent to it in the memory. Removing an item in the middle is problematic: you have to push *all* subsequent items one step back, or mark the removed item's memory space as "dead". Neither option is desirable. Similarly, adding an item causes you to push *all* subsequent items one step forward.

The Linked List

With **Linked Lists**, items are stored in a chain of cells that don't need to be at sequential memory addresses. Memory for each cell is allocated as needed. Each cell has a pointer indicating the address of the next cell in the chain. A cell with an empty pointer marks the end of the chain.

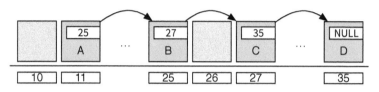

Figure 4.2 A Linked List in the computer's memory.

Linked lists can be used to implement Stacks, Lists, and Queues. There's no problem growing the list: each cell can be kept at any part of the memory. We can create lists as big as the amount of free memory we have. It's also easy to insert items in the middle or delete any item by changing the cell pointers:

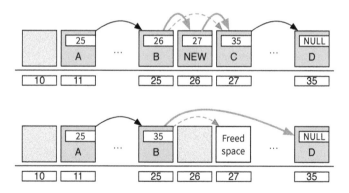

Figure 4.3 Adding an item between B and C; deleting C.

The Linked List also has its drawbacks: we can't instantly retrieve the nth item. For that, we have to start searching at the first cell, use it to get the address of the second cell, then get the second cell, use its pointer to the next cell and so on, until we get to the nth cell.

Also, if we're only given the address of a single cell, it's not easy to remove it or move backwards. With no other information, we can't know the address of the previous cell in the chain.

The Double Linked List

The **Double Linked List** is the Linked List with an extra: cells have two pointers: one to the cell that came before it, and other to the cell that comes after.

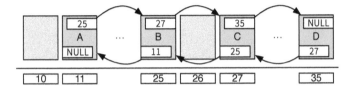

Figure 4.4 A double Linked List in the computer's memory.

It has the same benefits as the Linked List: no big chunk of memory preallocation is required, because memory space for new cells can be allocated on demand. And the extra pointers let us walk the chain of cells forwards *and* backwards. And if we're only given the address of a single cell, we're able to delete it.

Still, there's no way to access the nth item instantly. Also, storing two pointers in each cell directly translates to more code complexity and more required memory to store our data.

Arrays vs. Linked Lists

Feature-rich programming languages often come with built-in implementations for List, Queue, Stack and other ADTs. These implementations often resort to a default data structure. Some of these implementations can even switch data structures automatically during runtime, based on how data is being accessed.

When performance isn't an issue, we can rely on these generic ADT implementations and not worry about data structures. But when performance must be optimal, or when working with a lower level language that doesn't have such features, *you* must decide which data structures to use. Analyze the operations your data must undergo, and choose an implementation that uses an appropriate data structure. Linked Lists are preferable to Arrays when:

- You need insertions/deletions in the list to be extremely fast,
- You don't need random, unordered access to the data,
- You insert or delete items in the middle of a list,
- You can't evaluate the exact size of the list (it needs to grow or shrink throughout the execution).

Arrays are preferable over Linked Lists when:

- You frequently need random, unordered access to the data,
- You need extreme performance to access the items,
- The number of items doesn't change during execution, so you can easily allocate contiguous space of computer memory.

The Tree

Like the Linked List, the **Tree** employs memory cells that do not need to be contiguous in physical memory to store objects. Cells also have pointers to other cells. Unlike Linked Lists, cells and their pointers are not arranged as a linear chain of cells, but as a tree-like structure. Trees are especially suitable for hierarchical data, such as a file directory structure, or the command chain of an army.

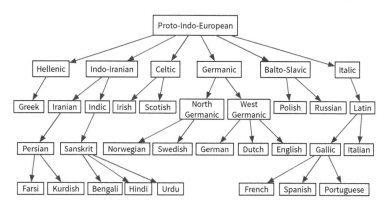

Figure 4.5 A tree with the origins of Indo-European languages.

In the Tree terminology, a cell is called a **node**, and a pointer from one cell to another is called an **edge**. The topmost node of a tree is the **Root Node**: the only node that doesn't have a parent. Apart from the Root Node, nodes in trees must have exactly *one* parent.[4]

Two nodes that have the same parent are siblings. A node's parent, grandparent, great-grandparent (and so on all the way to the Root Node) constitute the node's ancestors. Likewise, a node's children, grandchildren, great-grandchildren (and so on all the way to the bottom of the tree) are the node's descendants.

Nodes that do not have any children are **leaf nodes** (think of leaves in an actual tree 🌳). And a **path** between two nodes is a set of nodes and edges that can lead from one node to the other.

A node's **level** is the size of its path to the Root Node. The tree's **height** is the level of the deepest node in the tree. And finally, a set of trees can be referred to as a **forest**.

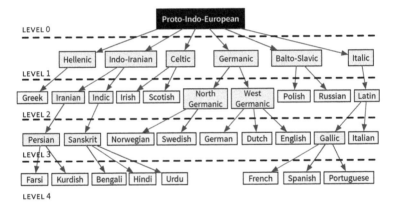

Figure 4.6 Leaves on this tree are present-day languages.

Binary Search Tree

A **Binary Search Tree** is a special type of Tree that can be efficiently searched. Nodes in Binary Search Trees can have at most two children. And nodes are positioned according to their value/key. Children nodes to the left of the parent must be smaller than the parent, children nodes to the right must be greater.

---

[4]If a node violates this rule, many search algorithms for trees won't work.

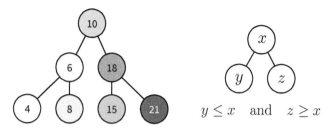

Figure 4.7   A sample binary search tree.

If the tree respects this property, it's easy to search for a node with a given key/value within the tree:

```
function find_node(binary_tree, value)
    node ← binary_tree.root_node
    while node:
        if node.value = value
            return node
        if value > node.value
            node ← node.right
        else
            node ← node.left
    return "NOT FOUND"
```

To insert an item, we search the value we want to insert in the tree. We take the last node explored in that search, and make its right or left pointer point to the new node:

```
function insert_node(binary_tree, new_node)
    node ← binary_tree.root_node
    while node:
        last_node ← node
        if new_node.value > node.value
            node ← node.right
        else
            node ← node.left
    if new_node.value > last_node.value
        last_node.right ← new_node
    else
        last_node.left ← new_node
```

TREE BALANCING If we insert too many nodes in a Binary Search Tree, we end up with a tree of enormous height, where many nodes have only one child. For example, if we insert nodes with keys/values always greater than the previous one, we end up with something that looks more like a Linked List. But we can rearrange nodes in a tree such that its height is reduced. This is called *tree balancing*. A perfectly balanced tree has the minimum possible height.

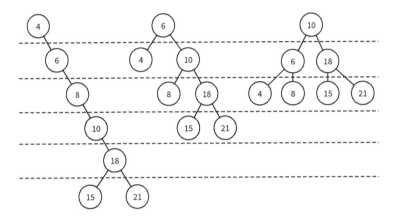

Figure 4.8 The same binary search tree in a very badly balanced form, in a somewhat balanced form, and in a perfectly balanced form.

Most operations with trees involve following links between nodes until we get to a specific one. The higher the height of the tree, the longer the average path between nodes, and the more times we need to access the memory. Therefore, it's important to reduce tree height. Building a perfectly balanced binary search tree from a sorted list of nodes can be done as follows:

```
function build_balanced(nodes)
    if nodes is empty
        return NULL
    middle ← nodes.length/2
    left ← nodes.slice(0, middle - 1)
    right ← nodes.slice(middle + 1, nodes.length)
    balanced ← BinaryTree.new(root=nodes[middle])
    balanced.left ← build_balanced(left)
    balanced.right ← build_balanced(right)
    return balanced
```

Consider a Binary Search Tree with n nodes. Its maximum height is n, in which case it looks like a Linked List. The minimum height, with the tree perfectly balanced, is $\log_2 n$. The complexity of searching an item in a binary search tree is proportional to its height. In the worst case, the search must descend to the lowest level, reaching all the way to the tree's leaves in order to find the item. Searching in a balanced Binary Search Tree with n items is thus $\mathcal{O}(\log n)$. That's why this data structure is often chosen for implementing Sets (which requires finding if items are already present) and Maps (which requires finding key-values).

However, tree balancing is an expensive operation, as it requires sorting all nodes. Rebalancing a tree after each insertion or deletion can greatly slow down these operations. Usually, trees are undergo balancing after several insertions and deletions take place. But balancing the tree from time to time is only a reasonable strategy for trees that are rarely changed.

To efficiently handle binary trees that change a lot, **self-balancing binary trees** were invented. Their procedures for inserting or removing items directly ensure the tree stays balanced. The **Red-Black Tree** is a famous example of a self-balancing tree, which colors nodes either "red" or "black" for its balancing strategy.[5] Red-Black Trees are frequently used to implement Maps: the map can be heavily edited in an efficient way, and finding any given key in the map remains fast because of self-balancing.

The **AVL Tree** is another breed of self-balancing trees. They require a bit more time to insert and delete items than Red-Black Trees, but tend to have better balancing. This means they're faster than Red-Black Trees for retrieving items. AVL Trees are often used to optimize performance in read-intensive scenarios.

Data is traditionally stored in magnetic disks that read data in big chunks. In these cases, the **B-Tree**, a generalization of Binary Trees, is used. In B-Trees, nodes may store more than one item and can have more than two children, making it efficient to operate with data in big chunks. As we'll soon see, B-Trees are commonly used in database systems.

---

[5] Self-balancing strategies are out of the scope of this book. If you are curious, there are videos on the Internet showing how they work.

The Binary Heap

The **Binary Heap** is a special type of Binary Search Tree, in which we can find the highest (or smallest) item instantly. This data structure is especially useful for implementing Priority Queues. In the Heap it costs $\mathcal{O}(1)$ to get the maximum (or minimum) item, because it is always the Root Node of the tree. Searching or inserting nodes still costs $\mathcal{O}(\log n)$. It has the same node placement rules as the Binary Search Tree, plus an extra restriction: a parent node must be greater (or smaller) than *both* its child nodes.

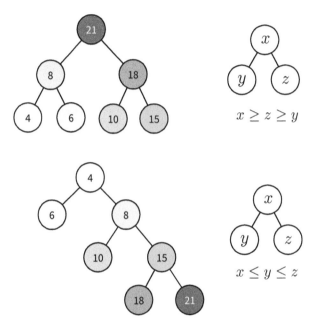

Figure 4.9 Nodes organized as a binary max-heap (top) and min-heap (bottom).

Remember to use the Binary Heap whenever you must frequently work with the maximum (or minimum) item of a set.

The Graph

The **Graph** is similar to the Tree. The difference is that there's no children or parent nodes, and therefore, no Root Node. Data is freely arranged as nodes and edges, and any node can have multiple incoming and outgoing edges.

This is the most flexible data structure there is, and it can be used to represent almost any type of data. For example, graphs are ideal for representing a social network, where nodes are people and edges represent friendships.

The Hash Table

The **Hash Table** is a data structure that allows finding items in $\mathcal{O}(1)$ time. Searching for an item takes a constant amount of time, whether you're searching among 10 million or just 10 items.

Similarly to the Array, the Hash requires preallocating a big chunk of sequential memory to store data. But unlike the Array, items are not stored in an ordered sequence. The position an item occupies is "magically" given by a **hash function**. That's a special function that takes the data you want to store as input, and outputs a random-looking number. That number is interpreted as the memory position the item will be stored at.

This allows us to retrieve items instantly. A given value is first run through the hash function. The function will output the exact position the item should be stored in memory. Fetch that memory position. If the item was stored, you'll find it there.

There is a problem with Hash Tables: sometimes the hash function returns the same memory position for two different inputs. That's called a **hash collision**. When it happens, both items have to be stored at the same memory address (for instance, by using a Linked List that starts at the given address). Hash collisions are an extra overhead of CPU and memory, so we try to avoid it.

A proper hash function will return random-looking values for different inputs. Therefore, the larger the range of values the hash function can output, the more data positions are available, and the less probable it is for a hash collision to happen. So we ensure at least 50% of the space available to the Hash Table is free. Otherwise, collisions would be too frequent, causing a significant drop in the Hash Table's performance.

Hash Tables are often used to implement Maps and Sets. They allow faster insertions and deletions than tree-based data structures.

However, they require a very large chunk of sequential memory in order to work properly.

Conclusion

We learned data structures provide concrete ways to organize data in computer memory. Different data structures require different operations for storing, deleting, searching, and running though stored data. There's no silver bullet: you should choose which data structure to use according to the situation at hand.

We learned that instead of using data structures directly in our code, it's better to use Abstract Data Types. This isolates your code from data manipulation details, and lets you easily switch the data structure of your programs without changing any of the code.

Don't reinvent the wheel by trying to create the basic data structures and abstract data types from scratch. Unless if you're doing it for fun, for learning, or for research. Use third-party data handling libraries that were already well tested. Most languages have built-in support for these structures.

Reference

- Balancing a Binary Search Tree, by Stoimen

    - See it at https://code.energy/stoimen

- Cornell Lecture on Abstract Data Types and Data Structures

    - See it at https://code.energy/cornell-adt

- IITKGP notes on Abstract Data Types

    - See it at https://code.energy/iitkgp

- Search Tree Implementation by "Interactive Python"

    - See it at https://code.energy/python-tree

CHAPTER 5

Algorithms

> [Coding is] attractive not only because it can be
> economically and scientifically rewarding, but
> also because it can be an aesthetic experience
> much like composing poetry or music.
>
> — DONALD KNUTH

ANKIND PURSUES SOLUTIONS to increasingly hard problems. Most times you come across a problem, many others have already worked on something similar. Chances are, they discovered efficient algorithms you can readily use. Searching for existing algorithms should always be your first move when solving problems.[1] In this chapter we'll explore famous algorithms that:

- 📜 Efficiently **sort** super long lists,
- 🔎 Quickly **search** for the item you need,
- 🕸 Operate and manipulate **graphs**,
- 🕵 Use WWII **operations research** to optimize processes.

You will learn to recognize problems on which you can apply these known solutions. There are many different types of problems: sorting data, searching patterns, route-finding, and more. And many types of algorithms are specific to fields of study: image processing, cryptography, artificial intelligence... We can't cover them all in this book.[2] Still, we'll learn some of the most important algorithms every good coder should be familiar with.

---

[1]Finding a new problem that hasn't been explored before is rare. When researchers find a new problem, they write a scientific paper about it.

[2]Here's a more comprehensive list: https://code.energy/algo-list.

5.1 Sorting

Prior to computers, sorting data was a major bottleneck that took huge amounts of time to perform manually. When the Tabulating Machine Company (that later became IBM) automated sorting operations in the 1890s, they sped up the US Census data compilation by several years.

Many sorting algorithms exist. The simpler ones are $\mathcal{O}(n^2)$. **Selection Sort** (sec. 2.1) is one such algorithm. It's the algorithm people tend to use for sorting a physical deck of cards. Selection Sort belongs to a big group of quadratic cost algorithms. We typically use them to sort small datasets of less than a thousand items. One notable quadratic sorting algorithm is **Insertion Sort**. It's very efficient at sorting nearly sorted datasets, even if they are huge:

```
function insertion_sort(list)
    for i ← 2 … list.length
        j ← i
        while j and list[j-1] > list[j]
            list.swap_items(j, j-1)
            j ← j - 1
```

Run this algorithm in pen and paper, using a nearly sorted list of numbers. For inputs where a negligible number of items are out of order, `insertion_sort` is $\mathcal{O}(n)$. In this case, it does less operations than any other sorting algorithm.

For large datasets which aren't nearly sorted, $\mathcal{O}(n^2)$ algorithms are too slow (see tbl. 3.2). In these cases, we need more efficient algorithms. The most famous efficient sorting algorithms are **Merge Sort** (sec. 3.6) and **Quicksort**, both $O(n \log n)$. Here's how Quicksort sorts a pile of cards:

1. If the pile has fewer than four cards, put them in the right order and you're done. Else, continue to step 2.
2. Choose at random any card from the pile to be **the pivot**.
3. Cards *larger* than the pivot go to a new pile to the *right*; cards *smaller* than the pivot go to a new pile to the *left*.
4. Start this procedure for each of the two piles you just created.
5. Join the left pile, pivot and right pile to get a sorted pile.

Shuffling a deck of cards and following these steps is a great way to learn Quicksort. That would also strengthen your understanding of recursion.

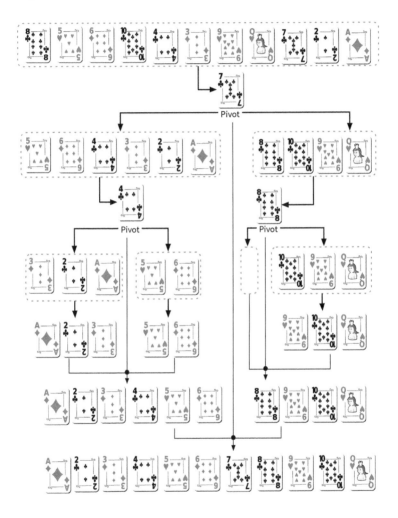

Figure 5.1 A sample Quicksort run.

You are now prepared to handle most problems that involve sorting. We didn't cover all sorting algorithms here, so remember there are many more, each suitable to specific sorting scenario.

5.2 Searching

Looking for specific information in memory is a key operation in computing. A sound knowledge of search algorithms is essential. The simplest search algorithm is **Sequential Search**: look at all items one after the other, until you find the one you want—or check *all* items to realize it's not there.

It's easy to see that Sequential Search is $\mathcal{O}(n)$, where n is the total number of items in the search space. But when the items we're searching are well structured, there are more efficient ways to search. We've seen in sec. 4.3 that data structured in a balanced binary search tree costs only $\mathcal{O}(\log n)$ to search.

If your items are structured in a sorted array, we can also search them in $\mathcal{O}(\log n)$ time through **Binary Search**. This search process discards half the search space in each step:

```
function binary_search(items, key):
    if not items
        return NULL
    i ← items.length / 2
    if key = items[i]
        return items[i]
    if key > items[i]
        sliced ← items.slice(i+1, items.length)
    else
        sliced ← items.slice(0, i-1)
    return binary_search(sliced, key)
```

Each step of `binary_search` does a constant number of operations and discards *half* the input. This means for n items, $\log_2 n$ steps fully reduce the input. As each step involves a fixed number of operations, the algorithm is $\mathcal{O}(\log n)$. You can search a million, or a trillion items, yet the search is still going to perform well.

Yet there's even more efficient. By storing your items in a Hash Table (sec. 4.3), you only need to calculate the hash of the key you are searching for. That hash gives the address of the item with the key! The time it takes to find an item *does not increase* when we increase the search space. It doesn't matter if you're searching among millions, billions or trillions of items—the number of operations is constant, meaning the process is $\mathcal{O}(1)$ in time. Almost instant.

5.3 Graphs

We've seen graphs are the flexible data structure that use nodes and edges to store information. They're widely used, to represent data like social networks (nodes are persons, edges are friendship relationships), telephone networks (nodes are telephones and stations, edges are communications), and much more.

Searching in Graphs

How do you find a node in a Graph? If the Graph's structure offers no navigation help, you must visit every node in the graph until you find the one you want. To achieve that, there are two approaches: depth-first and breadth-first.

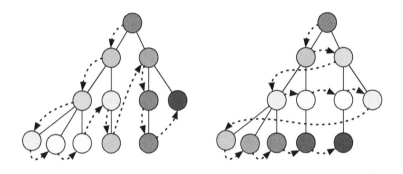

Figure 5.2   Exploring a graph depth-first versus breadth-first.

Searching a graph via **Depth First Search** (**DFS**), we keep following edges, going deeper and deeper into the graph. When we reach a node that has no edges to any new nodes, we go back to the previous node and continue the process. We use a Stack to keep track of the exploration trail, pushing a node when we explore it, and popping a node when we need to go back. The backtracking strategy (sec. 3.4) explores solutions this way.

```
function DFS(start_node, key)
    next_nodes ← Stack.new()
    seen_nodes ← Set.new()

    next_nodes.push(start_node)
    seen_nodes.add(start_node)

    while not next_nodes.empty
        node ← next_nodes.pop()
        if node.key = key:
            return node
        for n in node.connected_nodes
            if not n in seen_nodes
                next_nodes.push(n)
                seen_nodes.add(n)
    return NULL
```

If going deep in the graph isn't a good approach, you can try
Breadth First Search (**BFS**). It explores the graph level per level:
first the neighbors of your start node, then its neighbors' neighbors, and so on. To keep track of nodes to visit, we use a Queue.
Once we explore a node, we enqueue its children, then dequeue
the next node to explore.

```
function BFS(start_node, key)
    next_nodes ← Queue.new()
    seen_nodes ← Set.new()

    next_nodes.enqueue(start_node)
    seen_nodes.add(start_node)

    while not next_nodes.empty
        node ← next_nodes.dequeue()
        if node.key = key:
            return node
        for n in node.connected_nodes
            if not n in seen_nodes
                next_nodes.enqueue(n)
                seen_nodes.add(n)
    return NULL
```

Notice that **DFS** and **BFS** only differ in the way the next nodes to explore are stored: one uses a Queue, the other a Stack.

So which approach should we use? The DFS is simpler to implement and consumes less memory: you just need to store the parent nodes leading to the current node. In BFS you need to store the entire frontier of the search process. If you have a graph of million nodes, that might not be practical.

When you suspect the node you are searching isn't many levels away from the start, it's usually worth paying the higher cost of BFS, because you're likely to find the node faster. When you need to explore all the nodes of a graph, it's usually better to stick with DFS for its simple implementation and smaller memory footprint.

Figure 5.3   DFS, courtesy of http://xkcd.com.

You can see from fig. 5.3 that choosing the wrong exploration technique can have dire consequences.

Graph Coloring

Graph Coloring problems arise when you have a fixed amount of "colors" (or any other set of labels), and you must assign each node in the Graph a color. Nodes that are connected with an edge cannot share the same color. For instance, consider this problem:

> INTERFERENCE ⚠ You are given a map of cell phone towers and the neighborhoods they serve. Towers in adjacent neighborhoods have to operate on different frequencies to avoid interference. There are four frequencies to pick from. Which frequency do you assign to each tower?

The first step is to model this problem using a Graph. Towers are nodes in the graph. If two towers are close enough to cause interference, we connect them with an edge. Each frequency is a color.

How do you find a viable frequency assignment? Is it possible to find a solution that uses only three colors? Two colors? Finding the minimum number of colors of a valid color assignment is in fact an NP-complete problem—there are only exponential algorithms for it.

For this problem, we're not gonna show an algorithm. You should use what you learned so far and try solving this problem by yourself. You can do so at UVA,[3] an online judge that will test your proposed solution. It will run your code and tell you if it works. If it does, it will also rank your code's execution time against other people's code. Dive in! Research the algorithms and strategies for solving this problem, and try them. Reading a book can only take you so far. Submitting code to an online judge gives you the hands-on experience you need to become a great coder.

Path Finding

Finding the shortest path between nodes is the most famous graph problem. GPS navigation systems will search a graph of streets and crossroads to compute your itinerary. Some even use traffic data to increase the weight of edges representing jammed streets.

To find short paths, BFS and DFS strategies are usable but bad. One famous and very effective way of finding the shortest path is

---

[3]UVA's Graph Coloring Problem: https://code.energy/uva-graph-coloring

the **Dijkstra Algorithm**. As BFS uses an auxiliary Queue to keep track of nodes to explore, the Dijkstra Algorithm uses a Priority Queue. When new nodes are explored, their connections are added to the Priority Queue. A node's priority is the weight of the edges that take it to the starting node. This way, the next node to explore is always the closest to where we started.

There are cases where the Dijkstra Algorithm cycles forever without ever finding the destination node. A *negative cycle* can trick the search process to endlessly explore it. A negative cycle is a path in the graph that starts and ends at the same node, where the edge weights in the path sum to a negative value. If you are searching for a minimum path in a graph where edges can have negative weights, beware.

What if the graph you are trying to search is huge? **Bidirectional Search** can be used to increase search speed. Two search processes run simultaneously: one from the start node, the other from the destination node. When any node in one search area is also present in the other, *presto!* We've got the path. The search area involved in Bidirectional Search is twice smaller than the Unidirectional Search. Check out how the grey area is smaller than the yellow area:

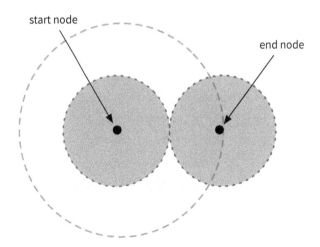

Figure 5.4 Unidirectional versus Bidirectional search areas.

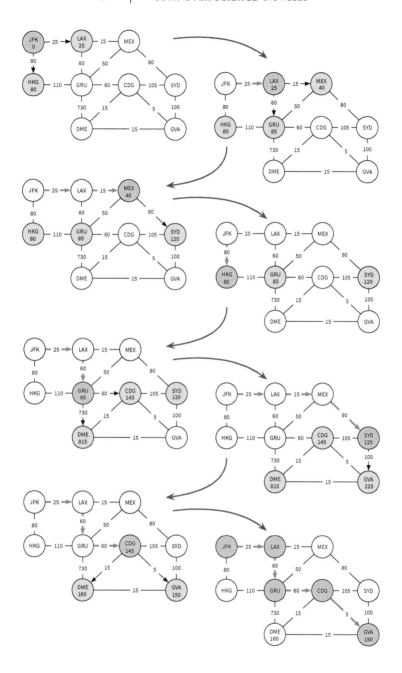

Figure 5.5 Finding the shortest route from JFK to GVA with Dijkstra.

PageRank

Did you ever wonder how Google is able to analyze billions of web pages and present you the most relevant ones? Many algorithms are involved, but the most important is the **PageRank Algorithm**.

Before founding Google, Sergey Brin and Larry Page were computer science academics at Stanford University, researching graph algorithms. They modeled the Web as a graph: web pages are nodes, and links between web pages are edges.

They figured if a web page receives many links from other important pages, then it must be important as well. They created the PageRank Algorithm after that idea. The algorithm runs in rounds. Each web page in the graph starts with an equal number of "points". After each round, each page distributes its points to the pages it has links to. The process is repeated until every score has stabilized. Each page's stabilized score is called its PageRank. By using the PageRank Algorithm to determine web page importance, Google quickly came to dominate other search engines.

The PageRank Algorithm can also be applied to other types of graphs. For example, we can model users of the Twitter network in a graph, and then calculate the PageRank of each user. Do you think users with a higher PageRank are likely to be important people?

5.4   Operations Research

During World War II, the British Army needed to make the best strategic decisions to optimize the impact of their operations. They created many analytical tools to figure out the best way to coordinate their military operations.

That practice was named **operations research**. It improved the British early warning radar system, and helped the United Kingdom better manage its manpower and resources. During the war, hundreds of Brits were involved in operations research. After, the new ideas were applied to optimize processes in businesses and industries. Operations research involves defining an objective to *maximize* or *minimize*. It can help maximize objectives like yield, profit, or performance; and minimize objectives like loss, risk, or cost.

For instance, operations research is used by airline companies to optimize flight schedules. Fine adjustments in workforce and equipment scheduling can save millions of dollars. Another example is in oil refineries, where finding the optimal proportions of raw materials in a blend can be seen as an operations research problem.

Linear Programming Problems

Problems where the objective and constraints can be modeled using linear equations[4] are called **linear programming problems**. Let's learn how these problems are solved:

> SMART FURNISHING 🗄 Your office needs filing cabinets. Cabinet X costs \$10, occupies 6 square feet and holds 8 cubic feet of files. Cabinet Y costs \$20, occupies 8 square feet and holds 12 cubic feet of files. You have \$140, and you can use up to 72 square feet in the office for the cabinets. What should you buy to maximize storage capacity?

First, we identify the variables of our problem. We're looking for number of cabinets of each type that should be bought, so:

- x: number of model X cabinets to purchase,
- y: number of model Y cabinets to purchase.

We want to maximize storage capacity. Let's call the storage capacity z, and model that value as a function of x and y:

- $z = 8x + 12y$.

Now we need to choose values of x and y that will yield the maximum possible z. These values must be chosen such that they respect our constraints in budget (less than \$140) and space (less than 72 square feet). Let's model these constraints:

- $10x + 20y \leq 140$ (budget constraint),
- $6x + 8y \leq 72$ (space constraint),
- $x \geq 0, y \geq 0$ (we can't buy a negative number of cabinets).

---

[4]Formally, polynomials with degree 1. They can have no squares (nor any powers) and their variables can only be multiplied by constant numbers.

How would you solve this problem? Simply buying as much of the model with the best storage/space ratio isn't the answer, because there's limited space in the office to hold cabinets. Maybe you'd go brute force: write a program that computes z for all possible x and y, and get the pair that produces the best z. This works for simple problems, but it's unfeasible to do it with many variables.

It turns out no coding is required to solve linear programming problems like this. You just need to use the right tool for the job: the **Simplex Method**. Simplex solves linear programming problems very efficiently. It has been helping industries solve complex problems since the 1960s. When you must solve a linear programming problem, don't reinvent the wheel: pick a ready-to-use Simplex solver.

Simplex solvers just require you to input the function that needs to be maximized (or minimized), along with the equations that model your constraints. The solver does the rest. Here, the choice for x and y that maximizes z is $x = 8$ and $y = 3$.

Simplex works through smart exploration of the space of acceptable solutions. To understand how Simplex works, let's represent all possible values for x and y in a 2D plane. Budgets and office space constraint are represented as lines:

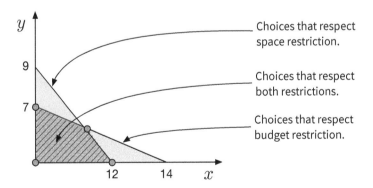

Figure 5.6 Values of x and y that satisfy the problem's constrains.

Note that the space of all possible solutions is a closed area in the graph. It has been proven that the optimum solution to a linear problem must be a corner point of this closed area—a point where lines representing constraints cross. Simplex checks these corner points and picks the one that optimizes z. It's not easy to visualize this process in linear programming problems that have more than two variables, but the mathematical principle works the same way.

Network Flow Problems

Many problems relating to networks and flows can be formulated in terms of linear equations, and thus be easily solved with Simplex. For instance, during the Cold War, the US Army mapped out the potential rail resupply routes the Soviets could use in Eastern Europe:

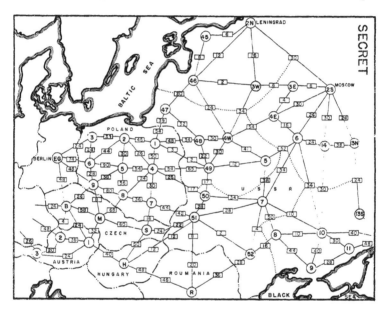

Figure 5.7 Declassified military report from 1955 of the Soviet rail network, showing the transportation capacity of its rail lines.

> SUPPLY NETWORK A rail network is represented by lines connecting cities. Each line has a maximum capacity: the largest daily flow of goods it can carry. What amount of supplies can be conveyed from a given producing city to a given consuming city?

To model the problem with linear equations, each rail line becomes a variable representing the amount of goods that should flow on the line. The constraints are: no rail line can convey more than its capacity; the incoming flow of goods must be equal to the outgoing flow of goods in all cities except the producing and consuming ones. We then pick values for our variables that maximize incoming goods in the receiving city.

We're not going to explain the mapping to linear form in detail. Our point here is just to let you know that many optimization problems involving graphs, cost, and flows can be solved easily with existing Simplex implementations. A lot of helpful documentation can be found online. Keep your eyes open and remember: don't lose time reinventing the wheel.

Conclusion

We showed there are several well known algorithms and techniques for solving all sorts of problems. The first step you should take when solving a problem is always looking for existing algorithms and methods.

There are many important algorithms we haven't included. For instance, we have more advanced search algorithms than the Dijkstra (such as the A⋆), algorithms for estimating how similar two words are (Levenshtein Edit Distance), machine learning algorithms, and much more…

Reference

- Grokking Algorithms, by Bhargava
    - Get it at https://code.energy/bhargava
- Introduction to Algorithms, by Cormen
    - Get it at https://code.energy/cormen
- Algorithms, by Sedgewick
    - Get it at https://code.energy/sedgewick
- Simple Linear Programming Model, by Katie Pease
    - Get it at https://code.energy/katie

CHAPTER 6

Databases

While I am best known for my work on databases, my fundamental skills are those of an architect: analyzing requirements and constructing simple, but elegant, solutions.

— CHARLES BACHMAN

MANAGING HUGE COLLECTIONS of data in computer systems is hard, but often vital. Biologists store and retrieve DNA sequences and their related protein structures. Facebook manages content generated by billions of people. Amazon keeps track of its sales, inventory, and logistics.

How do you store these big, constantly changing collections of data in disks? How do you let different agents retrieve, edit and add data at the same time? Instead of implementing these functionalities ourselves, we use a **DataBase Management System (DBMS)**: a special piece of software for managing databases. The DBMS organizes and stores the data. It mediates accesses and changes to the database. In this chapter, you'll learn to:

- Understand the **relational** model of most databases,
- Be flexible using **non-relational** database systems,
- Coordinate computers and **distribute** your data,
- Map stuff better with **geographical** database systems,
- Share data across systems thanks to data **serialization**.

Relational database systems are dominant, but non-relational database systems can often be easier and more efficient. Database systems are very diverse, and choosing one can be hard. This chapter provides a general overview of the different types of database systems out there.

Once data is easily accessible through a database system, it can be put to good use. A miner can extract valuable minerals and metals from a cheap looking rocky plot of land. Likewise, we can often extract valuable information from data. That's called **data mining**.

For instance, a big grocery chain analyzed its product-transaction data, and found that its top-spending customers often buy a type of cheese ranked below 200 in sales. Normally, they discontinued products with low sales. Data mining inspired managers not only to keep that cheese product, but to put it in more visible spots. That pleased their best customers, and made them come back even more. To be able to make such a smart move, the grocery chain had to have its data well organized in a database system.

6.1 Relational

The emergence of the **relational model** in the late 1960s was a huge leap for information management. Relational databases make it easy to avoid duplicate information and data inconsistencies. The majority of database systems used today are relational.

In the relational model, data is divided in different **tables**. A table works like a matrix or spreadsheet. Each data entry is a **row** in it. **Columns** are the different properties data entries can have. Usually columns impose a data type they can contain. Columns can also specify other restrictions: whether it's mandatory for rows to have a value in that column; whether the value in the column must be unique across all rows in the table, and more.

Columns are most commonly referred to as **fields**. If a column only allows whole numbers, we say it is an **integer field**. Different tables use different types of fields. The organization of a database table is given by its fields and the restrictions they enforce. This combination of fields and restrictions is called the table's **schema**.

All data entries are rows, and the database system won't accept a row into a table if it violates the table's schema. That's a big limitation of the relational model. When the characteristics of the data vary too much, fitting the data to a fixed schema can be troublesome. But if you're working with data of homogeneous structure, a fixed schema will help you ensure the data is valid.

Relationships

Imagine a database of invoices contained in a single table. For each invoice, we must store information about the order and the customer. When storing more than one invoice for the same customer, information gets duplicated:

Date	Customer Name	Customer Phone Number	Order Total
2017-02-17	Bobby Tables	997-1009	$93.37
2017-02-18	Elaine Roberts	101-9973	$77.57
2017-02-20	Bobby Tables	997-1009	$99.73
2017-02-22	Bobby Tables	991-1009	$12.01

Figure 6.1   Invoice data stored in a single table.

Duplicated information is hard to manage and update. To avoid it, the relational model splits related information in different tables. For instance, we divide our invoice data into two tables: "orders" and "customers". We make each row in the "orders" table reference a row in the "customers" table:

orders

ID	Date	Customer	Amount
1	2017-02-17	37	$93.37
2	2017-02-18	73	$77.57
3	2017-02-20	37	$99.73
4	2017-02-22	37	$12.01

customers

ID	Name	Phone
37	Bobby Tables	997-1009
73	Elaine Roberts	101-9973

Figure 6.2   Relationships between rows remove data duplication.

By relating data from different tables, the same customer can be part of many orders without data duplication. To support relationships, every table has a special identification field or ID. We use ID values to refer to a specific row within a table. These values must be unique: there can't be two rows with the same `ID`. The `ID` field of a table is also known as its **primary key**. A field that records references to other rows' `ID`s is called a **foreign key**.

With primary keys and foreign keys, we can create complex relationships between separate sets of data. For instance, the following tables store information about Turing Award winners:[1]

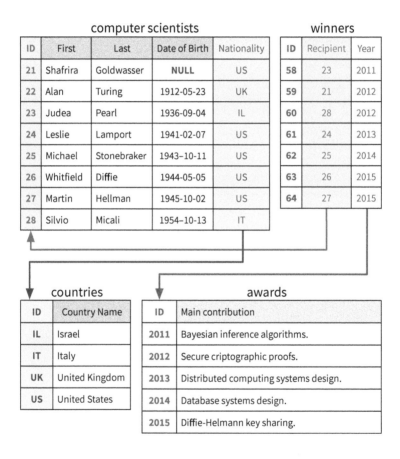

Figure 6.3 Computer scientists and Turing Awards.

---

[1]The Turing Award is like a Nobel Prize, but for computer science. It comes with one million dollars.

The relationship between computer scientists and awards isn't trivial like customers and orders. An award can be shared among two computer scientists—and nothing says a computer scientist can only win once. For this reason, we use a "winners" table just to store relationships among computer scientists and awards.

When a database is organized in a way that it is completely free of duplicate information, we say that the database is **normalized**. The process of transforming a database with replicated data to one without is called **normalization**.

Schema Migration

As an application grows and new features are added, it's unlikely its database structure (the schema of all its tables) remains the same. When we need to change the database structure, we create a **schema migration** script. It automatically upgrades the schema and transforms existing data accordingly. Typically, these scripts can also undo their changes. This allows to easily restore the database structure to match a past working version of the software.

There are ready-to-use schema migration tools for most DBMSs. They help you to create, apply, and revert schema migration scripts. Some big systems go through hundreds of schema migrations a year, so these tools are indispensable. Without creating schema migrations, your "manual" database changes will be hard to revert to a specific working version. It will be hard to guarantee compatibility between the local databases of different software developers. These problems occur frequently in big software projects with careless database practices.

SQL

Almost every relational DBMS works with a query language called **SQL**.[2] An in-depth SQL course is not in the scope of this book, but here you'll get a general idea of how it works. Having a small familiarity with SQL is important, even if you don't directly work with it. A SQL query is a statement of what data should be retrieved:

---

[2]SQL is more often pronounced *sequel*, but saying *ess-queue-ell* isn't incorrect.

```
SELECT <field name> [, <field name>, <field name>,…]
FROM <table name>
WHERE <condition>;
```

The items that come after **SELECT** are the fields that you want to get. To get all fields in the table, you can write "**SELECT** *". There can be several tables in the database, so **FROM** states which table you want to query. After the **WHERE** command, you state the criteria for selecting rows. Boolean logic can be used to specify multiple conditions. The following query gets all fields from a "customers" table, filtering rows by "name" and "age" fields:

```
SELECT * FROM customers
WHERE age > 21 AND name = "John";
```

You can query "**SELECT** * **FROM** customers" without specifying a **WHERE** clause. This causes every customer to be returned. There are also other query operators you should know: **ORDER BY** sorts the results according to the specified field(s); **GROUP BY** is used when you need to group the results in boxes and return per-box aggregated results. For instance, if you have a table of customers having a "country" and an "age" field, you could query:

```
SELECT country, AVG(age)
FROM customers
GROUP BY country
ORDER BY country;
```

This returns a sorted list of countries where your customers live, along with average customer age per country. SQL provides other aggregation functions. For instance, replace **AVG(age)** with **MAX(age)** and you get the oldest customer's age per country.

Sometimes, you need to consider information from a row and the rows it relates to. Imagine you have a table storing orders, and a table storing customers. The "orders" table has a foreign key for referencing customers (fig. 6.2). Finding information about customers who made high-valued orders requires fetching data from both tables. But you don't need to query the two tables individually and match records yourself. There's a SQL command for that:

```
SELECT DISTINCT customers.name, customers.phone
FROM customers
JOIN orders ON orders.customer = customers.id
WHERE orders.amount > 100.00;
```

That query returns the name and phone number of customers who made orders of over $100. The "SELECT DISTINCT" causes each customer to be returned only once. JOIN allows for very flexible querying,[3] but it comes at a price. Joins are expensive to compute. They may consider every combination of rows from the tables you are joining in your query. A database manager must always take into account the product of the number of rows of joined tables. For very large tables, joins become unfeasible. The JOIN is the greatest power and, at the same time, the major weakness of relational databases.

Indexing

For a table's primary key to be useful, we must be able to quickly retrieve a data entry when given its ID value. To that end, the DBMS builds an auxiliary **index**, mapping row IDs to their respective addresses in memory. An index is essentially a self-balancing binary search tree (sec. 4.3). Each row in the table corresponds to a node in the tree.

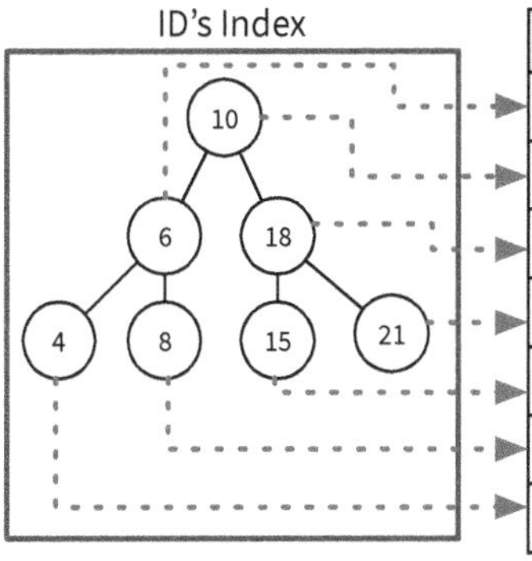

ID	Name	Date of Birth	Nationality
06	Barbara Liskov	1939-11-07	US
10	Peter Naur	1928-10-25	US
18	Adi Shamir	1952-07-06	IL
21	Ada Lovelace	1815-12-10	UK
15	Bill Gates	1955-10-28	US
08	Alan Turing	1912-06-12	UK
04	Dennis Ritchie	1941-09-09	US

Figure 6.4 An index mapping ID values to rows' locations.

---

[3]There are several ways to JOIN. See https://code.energy/joins for more.

Node keys are the values in the field we index. To find the register with a given value, we search for the value in the tree. Once we find a node, we get the address it stores, and use it to fetch the register. Searching a binary search tree is $\mathcal{O}(\log n)$, so finding registers in large tables is fast.

Usually, an index is created by the DBMS for each primary key in the database. If we often need to find registers by searching other fields (for instance, if we search customers by name), we can instruct the DBMS to create additional indexes for these fields too.

UNIQUENESS CONSTRAINTS Indexes are often automatically created for fields that have a uniqueness constraint. When inserting a new row, the DBMS must search the entire table to make sure no uniqueness constraint is violated. Finding if a value is present in a field without an index means checking all rows in the table. With an index, we can quickly search if the value we're trying to insert is already present. Indexing fields that have a uniqueness constraint is necessary to be able to insert items fast.

SORTING Indexes help to fetch rows in the indexed fields' sorted order. For instance, if there is an index for the "name" field, we can get rows sorted by name without any extra calculations. When you use `ORDER BY` in a field without an index, the DBMS has to sort the data in memory before serving the query. Many DBMSs might even refuse to fulfill queries asking to sort by a non-indexed field when the query involves too many rows.

If you must sort rows first by country and then by age, having an index on "age" or on "country" field doesn't help much. An index on "country" allows you to fetch rows sorted by country, but then you'll still need to manually sort items that have the same country by age. When sorting by two fields is required, **joint indexes** are used. They index multiple fields and won't help finding items faster, but they make returning data sorted by the multiple fields a breeze.

PERFORMANCE So indexes are awesome: they allow for super fast querying and instant sorted data access. Then why don't we have indexes for *all* fields in every table? The problem is when a new register is inserted to or removed from the table, all its indexes must be updated to reflect that. If there are a lot of indexes, updating, inserting or removing rows can become computationally expensive (remember tree balancing). Moreover, indexes occupy disk space, which is not an unlimited resource.

You should monitor how your application uses the database. DBMSs usually ship with tools to help you do that. These tools can "explain" queries, reporting which indexes a query used, and how many rows had to be sequentially scanned to perform a query. If your queries are wasting too much time sequentially scanning data in a field, add an index for that field and see how that helps. For example, if you are frequently querying a database for people of a given age, defining a index on the "age" field allows the DBMS to directly select rows corresponding to a given age. This way, you'll save time avoiding sequential scanning to filter rows that don't match the required age.

To adjust a database for higher performance, it's crucial to know which indexes to keep and which to discard. If a database is mostly read and rarely updated, it might make sense to keep more indexes. Poor indexing is a major cause for slowdown in commercial systems. Careless system administrators often won't investigate how common queries are run—they will just index random fields they "feel" will help performance. Don't do this! Use "explain" tools to check your queries and add indexes only when it makes a difference.

Transactions

Imagine a secretive Swiss bank ✚ keeps no records of money transfers: their database just stores account balances. Suppose someone wants to transfer money from his account to his friend's account in the same bank. Two operations must be performed on the bank's database: subtracting from one balance, and adding to another.

A database server usually allows multiple clients to read and write data simultaneously—executing operations sequentially would make any DBMS too slow. Here's the catch: if someone queries the total balance of all accounts *after* a subtraction is recorded but *before* the corresponding addition is, some money will be missing. Or worse: what if the system loses power between the two operations? When the system comes back online, it will be hard to find why the data is inconsistent.

We need a way for the database system to perform either *all* changes from a multi-part operation, or keep the data unchanged. To do this, database systems provide a functionality called **transactions**. A transaction is a list of database operations that must be executed **atomically**.[4] This makes the coder's life easier: the database system is responsible of keeping the database consistent. All the coder has to do is to wrap dependent operations together:

```
START TRANSACTION;
UPDATE vault SET balance = balance + 50 WHERE id=2;
UPDATE vault SET balance = balance - 50 WHERE id=1;
COMMIT;
```

Remember, performing multi-step updates without transactions eventually creates wild, unexpected, and hidden inconsistencies in your data.

6.2 Non-Relational

Relational databases are great, but have some limitations. As an application gets more complex, its relational database gets more and more tables. Queries become larger and harder to understand. And it requires more and more `JOIN`s, which are computationally expensive and can create serious bottlenecks.

The **non-relational model** ditches tabular relations. It hardly ever requires us to combine information from several data entries. Since non-relational database systems use query languages other than SQL, they are also referred to as **NoSQL databases**.

HOW TO WRITE A CV

Leverage the NoSQL boom

Figure 6.5 Courtesy of http://geek-and-poke.com.

---

[4]Atomic operations are performed in a single step: they can't half-execute.

Document Stores

The most widely known type of NoSQL database is the **document store**. In document stores, data entries are kept exactly the way they are needed by the application. The figure below compares the tabular way and the document way to store posts in a blog:

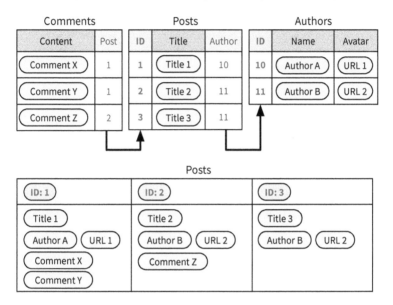

Figure 6.6 Data in the relational model (top) vs. NoSQL (bottom).

Notice how all the data about a post is copied into that post's register? The non-relational model *expects* us to duplicate information at each relevant place. It's hard to keep duplicated data updated and consistent. In return, by grouping relevant data together, document stores can offer more flexibility:

- You don't need to join rows,
- You don't need fixed schemas,
- Each data entry can have its own configuration of fields.

This means there are no "tables" and "rows" in document stores. Instead, a data entry is called a **document**. Related documents are grouped in a **collection**.

Documents have a primary key field, so relationships across documents are possible. But JOINs are not optimal on document stores. Sometimes they're not even implemented, so you have to follow relationships between documents on your own. Both ways, it's bad— if documents share related data, it should probably be replicated in the documents.

Like relational databases, NoSQL databases create indexes for primary key fields. You can also define additional indexes for fields that are often queried or sorted.

Key-Value Stores

The **key-value store** is the simplest form of organized, persistent data storage. It's mainly used for caching. For example, when a user requests a specific web page to a server, the server must fetch the web page's data from the database, and use it to render the HTML it will send to the user. In high-traffic websites, with thousands of concurrent accesses, doing that becomes impossible.

To solve this problem, we use a key-value store as a caching mechanism. The key is the requested URL, and the value is the final HTML of the corresponding web page. The next time someone asks for the same URL, the already generated HTML is simply retrieved from the key-value store using the URL as key.

If you repeat a slow operation that always produces the same result, consider caching it. You don't necessarily have to use a key-value store, you can store the cache in other types of databases. It's only when the cache is very frequently accessed that the superior efficiency of key-value store systems becomes relevant.

Graph Databases

In a **graph database**, data entries are stored as nodes, and relationships as edges. Nodes are not tied to a fixed schema and can store data flexibly. The graph structure makes it efficient to work with data entries according to their relationships. Here's how the information from fig. 6.6 would look in a graph:

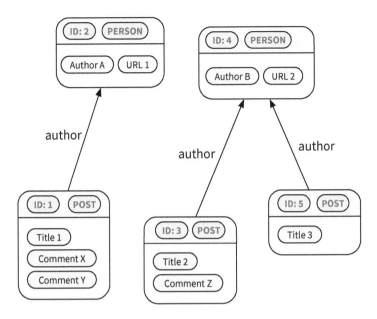

Figure 6.7 Blog information stored in a graph database.

This is the most flexible type of database. Letting go of tables and collections, you can store networked data in intuitive ways. If you wanted to map the subway and public bus stops of a city on a whiteboard, you wouldn't write tabular data. You would use cycles, boxes and arrows. Graph databases allow you to store data this way.

If your data looks like a network, consider using a graph database. They're especially useful when there are many important relationships between pieces of data. Graph databases also allow different types of graph-oriented queries. For example, storing public transportation data in a graph, you can directly query for the best one-legged or two-legged route between two given bus stops.

Big Data

The buzzword **Big Data** describes data-handling situations that are extremely challenging in terms of Volume, Velocity, or Variety.[5]

---

[5]Commonly known as the **three V's**. Some people make that five with Variability and Veracity.

Big data volume means you handle thousands of terabytes, as is the case of the LHC.[6] Big data velocity means you must store million of writes per second without holdups, or serve billions of read queries quickly. Data variety means that the data doesn't have a strong structure, so it's difficult to handle it using traditional relational databases.

Whenever you need a non-standard data management approach because of volume, velocity or variety, you can say it's a "Big Data" application. To run some state-of-the-art scientific experiments (such as the ones involving the LHC or the SKA[7]), computer scientists are already researching what they call **Megadata**: the storing and analyzing of millions of terabytes of data.

Big Data is often associated with non-relational databases, because of their added flexibility. It wouldn't be feasible to implement many types of Big Data applications with relational databases.

SQL vs NoSQL

Relational databases are data-centered: they maximize data structuring and eliminate duplication, regardless of how the data will be needed. Non-relational databases are application-centered: they facilitate access and use according to your needs.

We've seen NoSQL databases allow us to store massive, volatile, unstructured data fast and efficiently. Without worrying about fixed schemas and schema migrations, you can develop your solutions faster. Non-relational databases often feel more natural and easy to coders.

Your non-relational database will be powerful, but *you* will be responsible for updating the duplicated information across documents and collections. *You* will have to take the necessary measures to keep it consistent. Remember, with great power comes great responsibility.

---

[6]The Large Hadron Collider, or LHC, is the world's largest particle accelerator. During an experiment, its sensors generate 1,000 terabytes of data every second.

[7]The Square Kilometer Array, or SKA, is a collection of telescopes scheduled to start operations in 2020. It will generate a million terabytes of data each day.

6.3 Distributed

There are several situations in which not one, but several computers must act in coordination to provide a database system:

- Databases of several hundred terabytes. Finding a single computer with that much storage space is impractical.
- Database systems that process several thousand simultaneous queries per second.[8] No single computer has enough networking or processing power to handle such a load.
- Mission-critical databases, such as the ones recording altitude and speed of aircraft currently in a given airspace. Relying on a single computer is too risky—if it crashes, the database becomes unavailable.

For these scenarios, there are DBMSs that can run on several coordinated computers, forming a **distributed database** system. Now, let's see the most common ways to set up a distributed database.

Single-Master Replication

One computer is the **master** and receives all queries to the database. It is connected to several other **slave** computers. Each slave has a replica of the database. As the master receives write queries, it forwards them to slaves, keeping them synchronized:

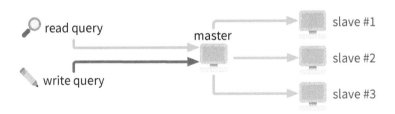

Figure 6.8 Single-master distributed database.

---

[8]Right after the final match in 2014's World Cup, Twitter experienced a peak of over 10,000 new tweets per second.

With this setup, the master is able to serve more read queries, because it can delegate those to the slaves. And the system becomes more reliable: if the master computer shuts down, the slave machines can coordinate and elect a new master automatically. That way, the system doesn't stop running.

Multi-Master Replication

If your database system must support a massive amount of simultaneous write queries, a single master cannot handle all the load. In this case, all computers in the cluster become masters. A load balancer is used to distribute incoming read and write queries equally among the machines in the cluster.

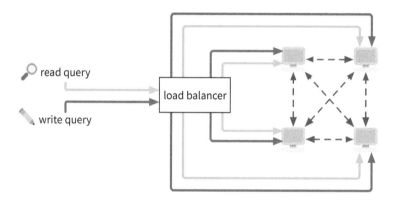

Figure 6.9   Multi-master distributed database.

Each computer is connected to all others in the cluster. They propagate write queries among themselves, so they all remain synchronized. Each has a copy of the entire database.

Sharding

If your database receives many write queries for large amounts of data, it's hard to synchronize the database everywhere in the cluster. Some computers might not have enough storage space to accommodate the entire thing. One solution is to partition the database among the computers. Since each machine owns a portion of the database, a query router forwards queries to the relevant one:

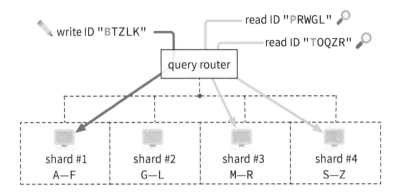

Figure 6.10 Sample sharding setup. Queries are routed according to the first letter in the ID being queried.

This setup can process many read and write queries for super huge databases. But it has a problem: if a machine in the cluster fails, the parts of data it is responsible for become unavailable. To mitigate that risk, sharding can be used with replication:

query router			
A—F	G—L	M—R	S—Z
master #1	master #2	master #3	master #4
slave 1.1	slave 2.1	slave 3.1	slave 4.1
slave 1.2	slave 2.2	slave 3.2	slave 4.2

Figure 6.11 A sharding setup with three replicas per shard.

With this setup, each shard is served by a master-slave cluster. This further increases the database system capacity to serve read queries. And if one of the main servers in a shard goes offline, a slave can automatically take its place, ensuring the system doesn't break down or lose data.

Data Consistency

In distributed databases with replication, updates made in one machine don't propagate instantly across all replicas. It takes some time until all machines in the cluster are synchronized. That can damage the consistency of your data.

Suppose you're selling movie tickets on a website. It has way too much traffic, so its database is distributed on two servers. Alice purchases a ticket on Server A. Bob is being served by Server B and sees the same free ticket. Before Alice's purchase propagates to Server B, Bob also purchases the ticket. Now the two servers have a **data inconsistency**. To fix it, you'll have to reverse one of the sales, and apologize either to an angry Alice or to an angry Bob.

Database systems offer tools to mitigate data inconsistencies. For instance, some allow you to issue queries that enforce data consistency across the entire cluster. However, enforcing data consistency reduces the performance of the database system. Transactions in particular can cause serious performance issues in distributed databases, as they force the coordination of all machines in the cluster to lock down potentially large sections of the data.

There is a trade-off between consistency and performance. If your database queries do not strongly enforce data consistency, they are said to work under **eventual consistency**. Data is guaranteed to *eventually* be consistent, after some time. This means some write queries might not be applied, and some read queries may return out-of-date information.

In many cases, working with eventual consistency won't cause problems. For instance, it's OK if a product you sell online shows 284 customer reviews instead of 285 because one was just made.

6.4 Geographical

Many databases store geographic information, such as the location of cities or the polygons that define state borders. Transportation applications might need to map out how the roads, rails and stations connect to each other. The Census Bureau needs to store the cartographic shape of thousands of census tracts, along with census data collected in each tract.

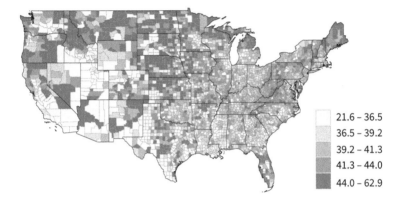

	21.6 – 36.5
	36.5 – 39.2
	39.2 – 41.3
	41.3 – 44.0
	44.0 – 62.9

Figure 6.12   Median age in the USA (data from census.gov).

In these databases, querying spatial information is interesting. For instance, if you're in charge of an emergency medical service, you need a database with the location of hospitals in the area. Your database system must be able to quickly answer which is the nearest hospital from any given location.

These applications ushered the development of special database systems, known as **G**eographical **I**nformation **S**ystems (**GIS**). They provide specially designed fields for geographical data: PointField, LineField, PolygonField, and so on. And they can perform spatial queries in these fields. On a GIS database of rivers and cities, you can directly order queries like *"list cities within 10 miles of the Mississippi river, ordered by population size"*. The GIS makes use of spatial indexes, so searching by spatial proximity is very efficient.

These systems even allow you to define spatial constraints. For instance, in a table storing land parcels, you can enforce the constraint that no two land parcels may overlap and occupy the same land. This can save land registry agencies a huge amount of trouble.

Many general-use DBMSs provide GIS extensions. Whenever you are dealing with geographical data, make sure you use a database engine with GIS support, and use its features to make smarter queries. GIS applications are often used in day-to-day life, for instance with GPS navigators like Google Maps or Waze.

6.5   Serialization Formats

How can we store data outside of our database, in a format that is interoperable across different systems? For instance, we might want to backup the data, or export it to an other system. To do this, the data has to go through a process called **serialization**, where it is transformed according to an encoding format. The resulting file can be understood by any system that supports that encoding format. Let's skim through a few encoding formats commonly used for data serialization.

SQL is the most common format for serializing relational databases. We write a series of SQL commands that replicate the database and all its details. Most relational database systems include a "dump" command to create an SQL-serialized file of your database. They also include a "restore" command to load such a "dump file" back to the database system.

XML is another way to represent structured data, but that doesn't depend on the relational model or to a database system implementation. XML was created to be interoperable among diverse computing systems, and to describe the structure and complexity of data. Some people say that XML was developed by academics who didn't realize their creation wasn't very practical.

JSON is the serializing format most the world is converging to. It can represent relational and non-relational data, in an intuitive way to coders. Many additions to JSON exist: BSON (Binary JSON) gives JSON maximum efficiency for data processing; JSON-LD brings the power of XML structure into JSON.

CSV or **C**omma **S**eparated **V**alues, is arguably the simplest format for data exchange. Data is stored in textual form, with one data element per line. The properties of each data element are separated by a comma, or some other character that doesn't occur in the data. CSV is useful for dumping simple data, but it gets messy to represent complex data using it.

Conclusion

In this chapter, we learned structuring information in a database is very important to make our data useful. We learned the different ways to do it. We've seen how the relational model splits data into tables, and how it gets linked back together with relationships.

Most coders only ever learn to work with the relational model, but we went beyond. We've seen alternative, non-relational ways to structure data. We discussed problems of data consistency, and how they can be mitigated using transactions. We discussed how to scale database systems to handle intense loads by using a distributed database. We've presented GIS systems, and the features they offer for working with geographic data. And we showed common ways to exchange data between different applications.

Lastly, unless you're just experimenting, pick a DBMS that is widely used. It will have fewer bugs and better performance. There are no silver bullets for database system selection. No specific DBMS will be the best pick for every scenario. Having read this chapter, you should understand the different types of DBMSs and their features, so you can make an informed choice of which to use.

Reference

- Database System Concepts, by Silberschatz

    – Get it at https://code.energy/silber

- NoSQL Distilled, by Sadalage

    – Get it at https://code.energy/sadalage

- Principles of Distributed Database Systems, by Özsu

    – Get it at https://code.energy/ozsu

CHAPTER 7

Computers

> Any sufficiently advanced technology
> is indistinguishable from magic.
>
> —ARTHUR C. CLARKE

COUNTLESS DIFFERENT MACHINES were invented to solve problems. There are many types of computers, from the ones embedded in robots roaming Mars to the ones powering the navigational systems of nuclear submarines. Almost all computers, including our laptops and phones, have the same working principle as the first computing model invented by Von-Neumann in 1945. Do you know how computers work under the hood? In this chapter, you'll learn to:

- ⅲ Understand foundations of computer **architecture**,
- 🐦 Choose a **compiler** to translate your code for computers,
- 🐑 Trade storage for speed with the **memory hierarchy**.

After all, coding has to look like magic to non-coders, not us.

7.1 Architecture

A computer is a machine that follows instructions to manipulate data. It has two main components: processor and memory. The memory, or **RAM**,[1] is where we write the instructions. It also stores the data to operate on. The processor, or **CPU**,[2] gets instructions and data from the memory and performs calculations accordingly. Let's learn how these two components work.

---

[1] Short for **R**andom **A**ccess **M**emory.
[2] Short for **C**entral **P**rocessing **U**nit.

Memory

The memory is divided into many cells. Each cell stores a tiny amount of data, and has a numerical address. Reading or writing data in memory is done through operations that affect one cell at a time. To read or write a specific memory cell, we must communicate its numerical address.

Since the memory is an electrical component, we transmit cell addresses through wires as binary numbers.[3] Each wire transmits a binary digit. Wires are set at higher voltage for the "one" signal or lower voltage for the "zero" signal.

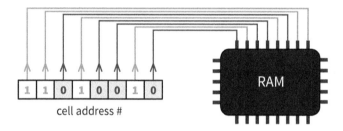

Figure 7.1 Informing the RAM to operate on cell # 210 (`11010010`).

There are two things the memory can do with a given cell's address: get its value, or store a new value. The memory has a special input wire for setting its operational mode:

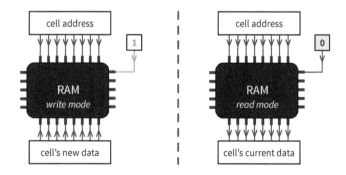

Figure 7.2 The memory can operate in read or write mode.

---

[3]Binary numbers are expressed in base 2. Appendix I explains how this works.

Usually, each memory cell stores an 8-digit binary number, which is called a **byte**. In "read" mode, the memory retrieves the byte stored in a cell, and outputs it in eight data-transmitting wires:

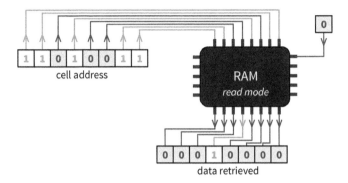

Figure 7.3 Reading the number 16 from memory address 211.

When the memory is in "write" mode, it *gets* a byte from these wires, and writes it to the informed cell:

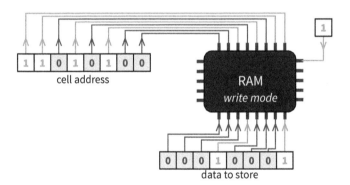

Figure 7.4 Writing the number 17 in memory address 212.

A group of wires used for transmitting the same data is a **bus**. The eight wires used to transmit addresses form the **address bus**. The other eight wires used to transmit data to and from memory cells form the **data bus**. While the address bus is unidirectional (only used to receive data), the data bus is bidirectional (used to send and receive data).

In any computer, CPU and RAM are constantly exchanging data: the CPU keeps on fetching instructions and data from memory, and occasionally stores outputs and partial calculations in it.

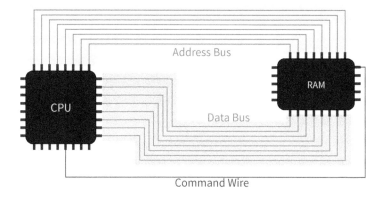

Figure 7.5   The CPU is wired to the RAM.

CPU

The CPU has some internal memory cells called **registers**. It can perform simple mathematical operations with numbers stored in these registers. It can also move data between the RAM and these registers. These are examples of typical operations a CPU can be instructed to execute:

- *Copy data from memory position #220 into register #3,*
- *Add the number in register #3 to the number in register #1.*

The collection of all operations a CPU can do is called its **instruction set**. Each operation in the instruction set is assigned a number. Computer code is essentially a sequence of numbers representing CPU operations. These operations are stored as numbers in the RAM. We store input/output data, partial calculations, and computer code, all mixed together in the RAM.[4]

---

[4]Code can even modify itself, by including instructions that rewrite parts of its code in RAM. Computer viruses often do that to make their detection by anti-virus software harder. That's an incredible parallel with biological viruses that change their DNA to hide from their hosts' immune system.

Figure 7.6 shows how some CPU instructions are mapped to numbers, as it appears in CPU manuals. As CPU manufacturing technology advanced, CPUs kept on supporting more operations. The instruction set of contemporary CPUs is huge. However, the most important operations already existed decades ago.

4004 Instruction Set
BASIC INSTRUCTIONS

MNEMONIC	OPR $D_3 D_2 D_1 D_0$	OPA $D_3 D_2 D_1 D_0$	DESCRIPTION OF OPERATION
NOP	0 0 0 0	0 0 0 0	No operation.
INC	0 1 1 0	R R R R	Increment contents of register RRRR.
ADD	1 0 0 0	R R R R	Add contents of register RRRR to accumulator with carry.
LD	1 0 1 0	R R R R	Load contents of register RRRR to accumulator.
LDM	1 1 0 1	D D D D	Load data DDDD to accumulator.
CLC	1 1 1 1	0 0 0 1	Clear carry.
IAC	1 1 1 1	0 0 1 0	Increment accumulator.
DAC	1 1 1 1	1 0 0 0	Decrement accumulator.

Figure 7.6 Part of Intel 4004's datasheet, showing how operations are mapped to numbers. It was the world's first CPU, released in 1971.

The CPU works in a never-ending loop, always fetching and executing an instruction from memory. At the core of this cycle is the PC register, or **Program Counter**.[5] It's a special register that stores the memory address of the next instruction to be executed. The CPU will:

1. Fetch the instruction at the memory address given by the PC,
2. Increment the PC by 1,
3. Execute the instruction,
4. Go back to step 1.

When the CPU is powered up, the PC is reset to its default value, which is the address of the first instruction to be executed by the machine. That's usually an immutable built-in program responsible for loading the computer's basic functionalities.[6]

---

[5] Don't confuse this with the common acronym for *Personal Computer*.

[6] In many personal computers, that program is called the BIOS.

After being powered up, the CPU keeps following this fetch-execute cycle until the computer shuts down. But if the CPU could only follow an ordered, sequential list of operations, it would be just a fancy calculator. The CPU is amazing because it can be instructed to write a new value to the PC, causing the execution to branch, or "jump" to somewhere else in the memory. And this branching can be conditional. For instance, a CPU instruction could say: *"set PC to address #200 if register #1 equals zero"*. This allows computers to execute stuff like this:

```
if x = 0
    compute_this()
else
    compute_that()
```

That's all there is to it. Whether you open a website, play a computer game, or edit a spreadsheet, computations are always the same: a series of simple operations which can only sum, compare, or move data across memory.

With many of these simple operations, we can express complicated procedures. For example, the code for the classic Space Invaders game has about 3,000 machine instructions.

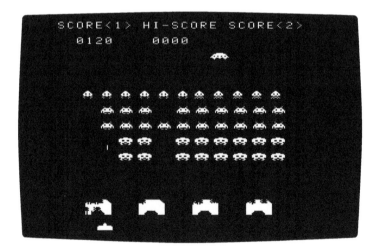

Figure 7.7 Space Invaders, released in 1978, is often considered the most influential video game ever.

CPU Clock Back in the 1980s, Space Invaders became super popular. People played it in arcade machines equipped with a 2 MHz CPU. That number indicates the CPU's **clock**: the number of basic operations it executes per second. With a two million hertz (2 MHz) clock, the CPU performs roughly two million basic operations per second. A machine instruction requires five to ten basic operations to complete. Hence, vintage arcade machines ran *hundreds of thousands* of machine instructions *every second*.

With modern technological progress, ordinary desktop computers and smartphones typically have 2 GHz CPUs. They can perform hundreds of millions machine instructions every second. And since recently, multi-core CPUs are hitting mass adoption. A quad-core 2 GHz CPU can execute close to a billion machine instructions per second. And it seems like our CPUs will be equipped with more and more cores in the future.[7]

CPU Architectures Ever wonder why you can't insert a PlayStation CD in your desktop computer and start playing the game? Or why you can't run iPhone apps on a Mac? The reason is simple: different CPU architectures.

Nowadays the x86 architecture is pretty standard, so a same code can be executed across most personal computers. However, cell phones, for example, have CPUs with different architectures that are more power-efficient. A different CPU architecture means a different CPU instruction set, thus a different way to encode instructions as numbers. Numbers that translate as instructions for your desktop CPU don't represent valid instructions for the CPU in your cell phone, and vice versa.

32-bit vs. 64-bit Architecture The first CPU, called Intel 4004, was built on a 4-bit architecture. This means it could operate (sum, compare, move) binary numbers of up to 4 digits in a single machine instruction. The 4004 had data and address buses with only four wires each.

---

[7]A CPU with 1,000 cores was already announced by researchers back in 2016.

Shortly afterwards, 8-bit CPUs became widely available. They were used in the early personal computers that ran DOS.[8] The Game Boy, a famous portable gaming computer in the 1980s and 1990s, also had an 8-bit processor. A single instruction in these CPUs can operate on eight-digit binary numbers.

Quick technological progress allowed the 16-bit, then the 32-bit architecture to become dominant. CPU registers were enlarged to accommodate 32-bit numbers. Larger registers naturally lead to larger data and address buses. An address bus with 32 wires allows addressing 2^{32} bytes (4 GB) of memory.

And our thirst for computing power raged on. Computer programs became more complex, and started using more memory. Four gigabytes of RAM became too little. And addressing over 4 GB of memory with numerical addresses that fit in 32-bit registers is tricky. This ushered the rise of the 64-bit architecture, which is dominant today. With 64-bit CPUs, extremely large numbers can be operated by the CPU in a single instruction. And 64-bit registers store addresses in a humongous memory space: 2^{64} bytes are over *17 billion* gigabytes.

BIG-ENDIAN VS. LITTLE-ENDIAN   Some computer designers thought it made sense to store numbers left-to-right in the RAM and CPU, in a way that is known as **little-endian**. Other computer designers preferred to write data in memory right-to-left, in what is known as **big-endian**. The binary sequence 1-0-0-0-0-0-1-1 can represent different numbers, depending on "endianness":

- Big-endian: $2^7 + 2^1 + 2^0 = 131$,
- Litte-endian: $2^0 + 2^6 + 2^7 = 193$.

Most CPUs today are little-endian, but there are a lot of big-endian computers out there. If data generated by a little-endian CPU needs to be interpreted by a big-endian CPU, we have to take measures to avoid **endianness mismatch**. Programmers manipulating binary numbers directly, particularly when parsing data that comes out of

---

[8]For **D**isk **O**perating **S**ystem. We'll explain operating systems soon.

network switches, should remember this. Even though most computers today are little-endian, Internet traffic standardized in big-endian, because most of the early network routers had big-endian CPUs. Big-endian data will appear garbled when read as little-endian, and vice versa.

EMULATORS Sometimes, it's useful to run in your own computer some code that was designed for a different CPU. That way, you can test an iPhone app without an iPhone, or play your favorite vintage Super Nintendo game. For these tasks, there are pieces of software called **emulators**.

An emulator mimics the target machine: it pretends to have the same CPU, RAM, and other hardware. The instructions are decoded by the emulator program, and executed within the emulated machine. As you can imagine, it's very complex to emulate a machine inside another one when they have different architectures. But since our computers are much faster than old ones, it's possible. You can get a Game Boy emulator, have your computer create a virtual Game Boy, and play the games just like you would on a physical Game Boy.

7.2 Compilers

We can program computers to perform MRIs, recognize our voices, explore other planets, and carry out many other complex tasks. It's remarkable that everything a computer can do is ultimately carried out through simple CPU instructions, that just sum and compare numbers. Complex computer programs, like a Web Browser, require millions or billions of such machine instructions.

But we rarely write our programs directly as CPU instructions. It would be impossible for a human to write a realistic 3D computer game this way. To express our orders in a more "natural" and compact way, we created **programming languages**. We write our code in these languages.[9] Then, we use a program called a **compiler** to translate our orders as machine instructions a CPU can run.

---

[9]We will learn more about programming languages in the next chapter.

To explain what a compiler does, let's image a simple mathematical analogy. If we want to ask someone to calculate the factorial of five, we can ask:

$$5! \ = \ ?$$

However, if the person we're asking doesn't know what a factorial is, that question won't make sense. We'd have to rephrase it using simpler operations:

$$5 \times 4 \times 3 \times 2 \times 1 \ = \ ?$$

What if the person we're asking can only perform sums? We'd have to simplify our expression even further:

$$5 + 5 + 5 + 5 + 5 + 5 + 5 + 5 + 5 + 5 + 5 + 5 +$$
$$5 + 5 + 5 + 5 + 5 + 5 + 5 + 5 + 5 + 5 + 5 + 5 \ = \ ?$$

As we write our calculation in simpler and simper forms, it takes more and more operations. It's the same with computer code. The compiler translates complex instructions in a programming language into a equivalent CPU instructions. Combined with the power of external libraries, we can express complex programs of billions of CPU instructions in relatively few lines of code that are easily understood and modified.

Alan Turing, the father of computing, discovered that simple machines can be powerful enough to compute *anything* that is computable. For a machine to have universal computing power, it must be able to follow a program containing instructions to:

- Read and write data in memory,
- Perform conditional branching: if a memory address has a given value, jump to another point in the program.

Machines that have such universal computing power are called **turing-complete**. It doesn't matter how complex or difficult a computation is, it can always be expressed in terms of simple read/write/branch instructions. With enough time and memory, these instructions can compute anything.

SOME GEEKS ARE SPOILSPORTS

Figure 7.8 Courtesy of http://geek-and-poke.com.

Recently, it was shown that a CPU instruction called "move" (MOV) is turing-complete. This means a CPU that can only perform the MOV instruction is capable of anything a full-fledged CPU is. In other words, any type of code can be expressed strictly by using MOV instructions.[10]

The important concept to get here is that if a program can be coded in a programming language, then it can be rewritten to run in any turing-complete machine, regardless of how simple it is. The compiler is the magic program that automatically translates code from a complex language into a simpler one.

---

[10]Check out this compiler that will compile any C code into MOV-only binary code: https://code.energy/mov.

Operating Systems

Compiled computer programs are essentially sequences of CPU instructions. As we learned, code compiled for a desktop computer won't run on a smartphone, because these machines have CPUs of different architectures. Still, a compiled program may not be usable on two computers that share the same CPU architecture. That's because programs must communicate with the computer's **operating system** to run.

To communicate with the world, programs must input and output stuff: open files, write a message on the screen, open a network connection, etc. But different computers have different hardware. It's impossible for a program to directly support all different types of screens, sound cards, or network cards.

That's why programs rely on an operating system to execute. With its help, programs can work effortlessly with different hardware. Programs make special **system calls**, requesting the operating system to perform required input/output operations. Compilers translate input/output commands into the appropriate system calls.

However, different operating systems often use incompatible system calls. The system call for printing something on the screen with Windows is different from the one used by Mac OS, or Linux.

That's why if you compile your program to run on Windows with a x86 processor, it won't work on a Mac with a x86 processor. Besides targeting a specific CPU architecture, compiled code also targets a specific operating system.

Compiler Optimizations

Good compilers work hard to optimize the machine code they generate. If they see parts of your code can be changed to a more efficient equivalent, they'll do it. Compilers may try to apply hundreds of optimization rules before producing a binary output.

That's why you shouldn't make your code harder to read in favor of micro-optimizations. In the end, the compiler will do all trivial optimizations anyway. For instance, one might argue this code:

```
function factorial(n)
    if n > 1
        return factorial(n - 1) * n
    else
        return 1
```

Should be changed into this equivalent:

```
function factorial(n)
    result ← 1
    while n > 1
        result ← result * n
        n ← n - 1
    return result
```

Yes, performing the **factorial** calculation without recursion uses less computational resources. Still there is no reason to change your code because of this. Modern compilers will rewrite simple recursive functions automatically. Here's another example:

```
i ← x + y + 1
j ← x + y
```

Compilers will avoid computing x + y twice by rewriting that:

```
t1 ← x + y
i ← t1 + 1
j ← t1
```

Focus on writing clean, self-explanatory code. If you have performance issues, use profiling tools to discover bottlenecks in your code, and try computing these parts in smarter ways. Don't waste time on unnecessary micromanagement.

There are situations, though, where we want to skip compilation. Let's see how to do that.

Scripting Languages

Some programming languages, called **scripting languages**, are executed without a direct compilation to machine code. These include JavaScript, Python, and Ruby. Code in these languages works by getting executed not directly by the CPU, but by an **interpreter** that must be installed in the machine that is running the code.

Since the interpreter translates the code to the machine in real time, it usually runs *much* slower than compiled code. On the other hand, the programmer can always run the code immediately, without waiting through the compilation process. When a project is very big, compiling can take hours.

Figure 7.9 "Compiling", courtesy of http://xkcd.com.

Google engineers had to constantly compile large batches of code. That made coders "lose" (fig. 7.9) a lot of time. Google couldn't switch to scripting languages—they needed the higher performance of the compiled binary. So they developed Go, a language that compiles incredibly fast, but still has a very high performance.

Disassembly and reverse engineering

Given a compiled computer program, it's impossible to recover its source code prior to compilation.[11] But it *is* possible to decode the

---

[11]At least for now. With the evolution of artificial intelligence, that could be possible some day.

binary program, transforming the numbers encoding CPU instructions into a human-readable sequence of instructions. This process is called **disassembly**.

We can then look at these CPU instructions and try to figure out what they're doing, in a process called **reverse engineering**. Some disassembly programs greatly help this process, automatically detecting and annotating system calls and frequently used functions. With disassembly tools, a hacker can understand every aspect of what a binary code does. I'm sure many of the top IT companies have secret reverse engineering labs, where they study their competitors' software.

Underground hackers often analyze the binary code from licensed programs like Windows, Photoshop, and Grand Theft Auto, in order to determine which part of the code verifies the license. They modify the binary code, placing an instruction to directly JUMP to the part of the code that executes after the license has been validated. When the modified binary is run, it gets to the injected JUMP command before the license is even checked, so people can run these illegal, pirated copies without paying.

Security researchers and engineers working for secret governmental spying agencies also have labs to study popular consumer software like iOS, Windows, or Internet Explorer. They identify potential security breaches in these programs, to defend people from cyber attacks or to hack into high-value targets. The most famous attack of this kind was the Stuxnet, a cyberweapon built by agencies from United States and Israel. It slowed down Iran's nuclear program by infecting computers that controlled underground Iranian fusion reactors.

Open-Source Software

As we explained earlier, from the binary executable you can analyze the raw instructions for the program in question, but you can't recover the original source code that was used to generate the binary.

Without the original source code, even though you can change the binary a little bit to hack it in small ways, it's practically impossible to make any major change to the program, such as adding a new feature. Some people believe that it's much better to build code collaboratively, so they started to make their source code open for other people to change. That's the main concept about open source: software that everyone can use and modify freely. Linux-based operating systems (such as Ubuntu, Fedora, Debian) are open-source, whereas Windows and Mac OS are closed source.

An interesting asset of open-source operating systems is that everyone can inspect the source code to look for security vulnerabilities. It was already confirmed that governmental agencies have exploited and spied on millions of civilians using unpatched security breaches in every-day consumer software.

With open-source software, there are more eyes on the code, so it's harder for malicious third parties and government agencies to insert surveillance backdoors. When using Mac OS or Windows, you have to trust that Apple or Microsoft aren't compromising your security and are doing their best to prevent any severe security flaw. Open-source systems are open to public scrutiny, so there are less chances that security flaws slip through unnoticed.

7.3   Memory Hierarchy

We know a computer works by having its CPU execute simple instructions. We know these instructions can only operate on data stored in CPU registers. However, their storage space is usually limited to less than a thousand bytes. This means CPU registers constantly have to transfer data to and from the RAM.

If memory access is slow, the CPU has to sit idle, waiting for the RAM to do its work. The time it takes to read and write data in memory is directly reflected in computer performance. Increasing memory speed can boost your computer as much as increasing CPU speed. Data in CPU registers is accessed near-instantly by the CPU, within just *one* cycle.[12] The RAM, however, is *way* slower.

---

[12]In a CPU with a 1 GHz clock, a cycle lasts about a billionth of a second—the time it takes for light to travel from this book to your eyes.

Processor-Memory Gap

Recent technological developments increased CPU speeds expo-
nentially. Memory speeds also increased, but at a much slower
rate. This performance gap between CPU and RAM is known as the
Processor-Memory Gap: CPU instructions are "cheap" as we can
execute plenty of them, whereas getting data from the RAM takes
a lot more time, so it's "expensive". As this gap became wider, the
importance of efficient memory access grew even more.

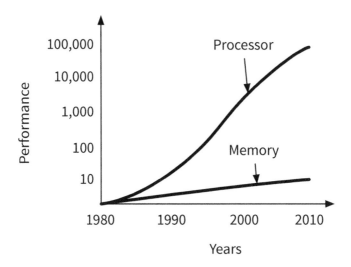

Figure 7.10 The processor-memory gap in the last decades.

In modern computers, it takes about a *thousand* CPU cycles to get
data from the RAM—about 1 microsecond.[13] That's incredibly fast,
but it's an eternity compared to the time it takes to access CPU
registers. Computer scientists started to try to find ways to reduce
the number of RAM operations required by their computations.

---

[13]It takes about ten microseconds for sound waves from your voice to reach a
person that's in front of you.

Temporal and Spatial Locality

When trying to minimize RAM access, computer scientists started noticing two things:

- **Temporal Locality**: when a memory address is accessed, it's probable it will be accessed again soon.
- **Spatial Locality**: when a memory address is accessed, it's probable addresses that are adjacent to it are going to be accessed soon.

It would be great to store these memory addresses in CPU registers in anticipation. That would avoid most of the expensive RAM operations. However, industry engineers found no viable way to design CPU chips with enough internal registers. Still, they found a great way to explore temporal and spatial locality. Let's see how this works.

The L1 Cache

It's possible to build an extremely fast auxiliary memory, integrated with the CPU. We call it the **L1 cache**. Getting data from this memory into the registers is just a tiny bit slower than getting data from the registers themselves.

With an L1 cache, we can copy the contents of memory addresses with high probability of being accessed close to the CPU registers. This way, they can be very quickly loaded into CPU registers. It takes only about ten CPU cycles to get data from the L1 cache into the registers. That's about a hundred times faster then fetching it from the RAM.

With about 10 KB of L1 cache memory and smart utilization of temporal and spatial locality, over half of RAM access calls can be fulfilled by the cache alone. This innovation revolutionized computing technology. Equipping a CPU with an L1 cache drastically reduces the time it has to wait for data. The CPU gets to spend much more time doing actual computations rather than sitting idle.

The L2 Cache

Increasing the size of the L1 cache would make fetching data from the RAM an even rarer operation, further reducing CPU waiting time. However, growing the L1 cache without slowing it down is difficult. After the L1 cache is about 50 KB in size, further increasing it gets very expensive. The better solution is to build an additional memory cache: the **L2 cache**. By allowing it to be slower, it can be much larger than the L1 cache. A modern CPU will have about 200 KB of L2 cache. It takes about a hundred CPU cycles to get data from the L2 cache into CPU registers.

We keep the very highly likely accessed addresses copied in the L1 cache. Memory spaces with a pretty high probability of being accessed are copied to the L2 cache. If a memory address isn't copied in the L1 cache, the CPU can still try the L2 cache. Only if it's in neither cache does it have to access the RAM.

Many manufacturers are now shipping processors with an L3 cache: larger and slower than the L2, but still faster than the RAM. The L1/L2/L3 caches are so important they take up most of the silicon space inside a CPU chip.

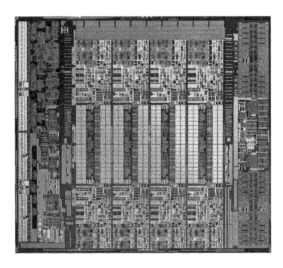

Figure 7.11 Microscope photo of an Intel Haswell-E processor. The square structures in the center are 20 MB of L3 cache.

The use of L1/L2/L3 caches dramatically increase the performance of computers. With an L2 cache of 200 KB, less than 10% of memory requests made by the CPU have to be fetched directly from the RAM.

Next time you go buy a computer, remember to compare the different sizes of L1/L2/L3 caches of the CPUs you're looking at. Better CPUs will have larger caches. It's often better to get a CPU with a slower clock but larger cache.

Primary Memory vs. Secondary Memory

As you can see, a computer has different types of memories, arranged in a hierarchy. The top-performing memories are limited in size and very expensive. As we go down the hierarchy, more memory space is available, but at lower access speeds.

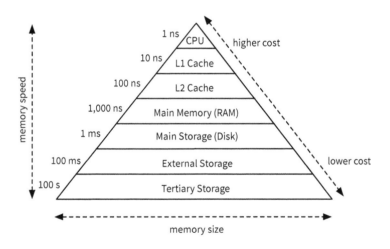

Figure 7.12 Memory hierarchy diagram.

After CPU registers and caches, next down the memory hierarchy is the **RAM**. It's responsible for storing data and code of all currently running processes. As of 2017, a computer usually has 1 to 10 GB of RAM. In many cases, that might not be enough to fit the computer's operating system along with all other running programs.

In these cases, we have to dig deeper in the memory hierarchy, and use the **hard disk**. As of 2017, computers usually have hard disks of hundreds of gigabytes—more than enough to fit data from all currently running programs. When the RAM is full, we move its currently idle data to the hard disk to free up some memory.

The problem is, hard disks are *extremely* slow. Typically, it takes a **million** CPU cycles, or a millisecond[14] to move data between the disk and the RAM. It might seem that accessing the data from the disk is fast, but remember: accessing the RAM only takes a thousand cycles—the disk takes *a million*. The RAM memory is often called **primary memory**, whereas programs and data stored in the disk are said to be in **secondary memory**.

The CPU cannot directly access secondary memory. Prior to execution, programs stored in the secondary memory must be copied to the primary memory. In fact, each time you boot your computer, *even* your operating system has to be copied from the disk to the RAM before the CPU can run it.

NEVER EXHAUST THE RAM It's important to ensure all the data and programs a computer handles during typical activity can fit in its RAM. Otherwise, the computer will constantly transfer data between the disk and RAM. Since that operation is *very* slow, the computer's performance will degrade *so much* it will become useless. In this scenario, the computer spends more time waiting for data to travel than doing actual computations.

When a computer is constantly getting data from the disk into RAM, we say that it's in **thrashing mode**. Servers must always be monitored: if they start processing stuff that cannot fit into the RAM, thrashing might cause the whole server to crash. That's what will cause a long line forming in a bank or at a cash register, while the attendant can do little but blame the thrashing computer system. Insufficient RAM is possibly one of the main causes of server failure.

---

[14]A standard photograph captures light during about about four milliseconds.

External and Tertiary Storage

The memory hierarchy goes further down. If connected to a network, a computer can access memory managed by other computers, either in the local network or on the Internet (aka *in the cloud*). But that takes even more time: while reading a local disk takes a millisecond, getting data from a network can take hundreds of milliseconds. It takes about ten milliseconds just for a network packet to travel from one computer to an other. If the network packet goes through the Internet, it often travels for much longer: two to three hundred milliseconds—the same duration as the blink of an eye. ☺

In the bottom of the memory hierarchy, we have **tertiary storage**: storage devices that are not always online and available. We can affordably store dozens of millions of gigabytes of data in magnetic tape cartridges or CDs. Accessing data in this medium however, requires someone to pick up the medium and insert it in a reader device. That can take minutes or days.[15] Tertiary storage is only suitable for archiving data you'll rarely need to access.

Trends in Memory Technology

It has been hard to significantly improve technology used in "fast" memories (the ones on top of the memory hierarchy). On the other hand, "slow" memories are getting faster and cheaper. The cost of hard disk storage has been dropping for decades, and it seems this trend will continue.

New technologies are also making disks faster. We're switching from magnetic spinning disks to Solid State Drives (SSD). The absence of moving parts allows them to be faster, more reliable, and less power-hungry.

Disks with SSD technology are getting cheaper and faster everyday, but they're still expensive. Some manufacturers are producing hybrid disks with both SSD and magnetic technology. The frequently accessed data is stored in the SSD, and the less frequently accessed data is kept in the slower magnetic part. When the less accessed data starts to be frequently accessed, it's copied into the

---

[15]Try asking the IT department to backup magnetic tapes on a Friday night...

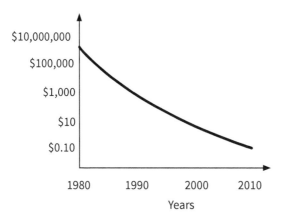

Figure 7.13   Disk storage cost per gigabyte.

fast SSD part of the hybrid drive. It's similar to the trick CPUs use to quicken RAM access through internal caches.

Conclusion

In this chapter, we explained some very basic aspects of how computers work. We've seen that *anything* that is computable can be expressed in terms of simple instructions. We learned there is a program called the compiler, that translates our complex computational commands to simple instructions that a CPU can do. Computers can do complex computations simply because of the massive amount of basic operations their CPUs can do.

We learned our computers have fast processors, but relatively slow memory. But the memory is accessed not at random, but according to spatial and temporal locality. That allows using faster memories to cache memory data that has a high access probability. We've seen this principle applied in several levels of caching: from the L1 cache all the way down to tertiary storage.

The caching principle discussed in this chapter can be applied to many scenarios. Identifying parts of data more frequently used by your application and making this data faster to access is one of the most used strategies to make computer programs run faster.

Reference

- Structured Computer Organization, by Tanenbaum
    - Get it at https://code.energy/tanenbaum
- Modern Compiler Implementation in C, by Appel
    - Get it at https://code.energy/appel

Chapter 8

Programming

> When someone says: "I want a programming language in which I need only say what I wish done", give him a lollipop.
>
> —Alan J. Perlis

W E WANT COMPUTERS to understand us. This is why we express our orders in a programming language: a language the machine will understand. Unless you hire a coder, or you are in a science fiction movie, you can't just tell a computer what to do in Shakespearean English. For now, only coders have the power to instruct a machine on what to do without constraints. And as your knowledge of programming languages deepens, your power as a coder grows. In this chapter, you'll learn to:

- ㊙ Spot the secret **linguistics** that govern code,
- x Store your precious information inside **variables**,
- Think solutions under different **paradigms**.

We won't get into the syntactical and grammatical formalities of computer science. Relax and read on!

8.1 Linguistics

Programming languages differ wildly, but all of them exist to do one thing: manipulate information. These languages rely on three basic building blocks to do this. A **value** represents information. An **expression** produces a value. A **statement** uses a value to give an instruction to a computer.

Values

The kind of information a value can encode varies from language to language. In the most rudimental languages, a value can only encode very simple information, such as an integer or a floating point[1] number. As languages grew more complex, they started to handle characters, and later strings, as values. In C, which is still a very low level language, you can define a structure: a way to define values that are composed from groups of other values. For instance, you could define a value type called "coordinate", that would be made of two floats: latitude and longitude.

Values are so important, that they are also known as a programming language's "first-class citizens". Languages allow all sorts of operations with values: they can be created at runtime, can be passed as arguments to functions, and be returned by functions.

Expressions

You can create a value in two ways: either by writing a **literal**, or by calling a **function**. Here's an example expression of a literal:

```
3
```

Boom. We literally just created the value 3 by writing **3**. Pretty straightforward. Other types of values can also be created as literals. Most programming languages will allow you to create the string value *hello world* by typing **"hello world"**. Functions, on the other hand, will generate a value following a method or procedure that's coded somewhere else. For example:

```
getPacificTime()
```

This expression created a value equal to the current time in Los Angeles. If it's 4 a.m., the method returned 4.

Another basic element in every programming language is the **operator**. An operator can join simple expressions to form more complex ones. For example, using the + operator, we can create a value equal to the time in New York:

---

[1]Floating points are a common way to represent numbers that have a decimal.

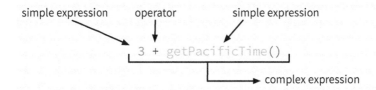

When it's 4 a.m. in Los Angeles, our expression reduces to 7. In fact, an expression is anything you write that the computer will be able to reduce to a single value. Big expressions can be combined with other expressions through operators, forming even larger expressions. In the end, even the most complex expression must always evaluate to a single value.

Alongside literals, operators and functions, expressions can also contain parentheses. Parentheses allows control over **operator precedence**: $(2 + 4)^2$ evaluates to 6^2, which in turn evaluates to 36. The expression $2 + 4^2$ evaluates to $2 + 16$, then to 18.

Statements

While an expression is used to represent a value, a statement is used to instruct the computer to *do* something. For example, this statement causes a message to be shown: `print("hello world")`.

Figure 8.1   Courtesy of http://geek-and-poke.com.

More complex examples include the *if, while-loop* and *for-loop* statements. Different programming languages support different types of statements.

DEFINITIONS Programming languages have special statements, called **definitions**. They change the state of a program by adding an entity that didn't exist, like a new value or function.[2] To refer to an entity we defined, we need to associate a name to it. That's called **name binding**. For example, the name `getPacificTime` had to be bound to a function definition somewhere.

8.2 Variables

Variables are the most important name binding there is: the one between a name and a value. A variable associates a name to the memory address where a value is stored, serving as an "alias". Most often, a variable is created using the assignment operator. In this book's pseudocode, assignments are written ←, like this:

```
pi ← 3.142
```

In most programming languages, assignments are written =. Some languages even require you to *declare* a name as a variable, before it is defined. You'll end up with something like this:

```
var pi
pi = 3.142
```

This statement reserves a memory block, writes the value **3.142** in it, and associates the name "**pi**" to the memory block's address.

Variable Typing

In most programming languages, variables must have an assigned type (e.g. integer, float, or string). This way, the program knows how it should interpret the 1s and 0s it reads in the variable's memory block. This helps to spot errors when operating with our vari-

---

[2]Sometimes, entities can be imported from pre-coded external libraries.

ables. If a variable is of the "string" type, while an other is of the integer type, it makes no sense to sum them.

There are two ways to perform type checking: statically and dynamically. Static type checking requires the coder to declare the type of every variable before using it. For example, programming languages like C and C++ will have you write:

```
float pi;
pi = 3.142;
```

This declares that the variable named pi can only store data that represents a floating point number. Statically typed languages can apply extra optimizations while compiling the code, and detect possible bugs even before you execute the code. However, declaring types every time you use a variable can get boring.

Some languages prefer checking types dynamically. With dynamic type checking, any variable can store any type of value, so no type declaration is required. However, when the code is executing, extra type checking is performed when operating with variables, to ensure operations between variables all make sense.

Variable Scope

If all name bindings were available and valid at all points in the program, programming would be extremely difficult. As programs get bigger, the same names of variables (such as time, length, or speed) might end up being used in unrelated parts of the code.

For example, I could define a "length" variable in two points in my program without noticing, and that would cause a bug. Worse yet, I could import a library that also uses a "length" variable: in this case the length from my code would collide with the length from the imported code.

To avoid collisions, names bindings are not valid over the entire source code. The variable's **scope** defines where it is valid and can be used. Most languages are set up such that a variable is only valid within the function where it was defined.

The current **context**, or **environment**, is the set of all name bindings that are available in a program at a given point. Usually, variables that are defined within a context are instantly deleted and freed from the computer's memory once the execution flow leaves that context. Though it's not recommended, you can bypass this rule and create variables that are always accessible *anywhere* in your program. These are called **global variables**.

The collection of all names available globally consists of your **namespace**. You should watch the namespace of your programs closely. It should be kept as small as possible. In large namespaces, it's easier to create name conflicts.

When adding more names to your program's namespace, try to minimize the number of names added. For example, when you import an external module, only add the names of the functions you are going to use. Good modules should require the user to add the very little to their namespace. Adding unnecessary things to the namespace causes a problem known as **namespace pollution**.

8.3   Paradigms

A **paradigm** is a specific collection of concepts and practices that define a field of science. A paradigm will orientate how you approach a problem, the techniques you use, and the structure of your solution. For instance, Newtonian and Relativistic schools are two different paradigms of physics.

For both coding and physics, the way you approach your problems changes completely depending on the paradigm you consider. A **programming paradigm** is a point of view of the coding realm. It will direct your coding style and technique.

You can use one or multiple paradigms in your program. It's best to use the paradigms that the programming language you are using is based on. In the 1940s, the first computers were manually programmed by flipping switches to insert 1s and 0s into the computer's memory. Programming never stopped evolving, and paradigms emerged to empower people to code with more efficiency, complexity and speed.

There are three main programming paradigms: imperative, declarative, and logic. Unfortunately, most coders only learn how to properly work with the first one. Knowing about all three is important, because it will enable you to benefit from the features and opportunities each programming language offers. This way, you'll be able to code with maximum effectiveness.

Imperative Programming

The **imperative programming paradigm** is about instructing the computer on what it must do exactly at each step using specific commands. Each command changes the computer's state. The sequence of commands that constitutes a program is followed, one after another.

This was the first programming paradigm, as it's a natural extension of the way our computers work. Computations are always performed by CPU instructions that are executed one after another. In the end, every computer program is ultimately executed by computers under this paradigm.

Imperative Programming is by far the most widely known paradigm. In fact, many programmers are familiar only with this one. It's also a natural extension of the way humans work: we use this paradigm to describe a cooking recipe, a car repair routine, and other everyday procedures. When we are lazy about doing a boring task, we code these instructions into a program and a computer does it for us. Programmer laziness is responsible for many important things.

Figure 8.2 "The General Problem", from http://xkcd.com.

MACHINE CODE PROGRAMMING Early programmers, who had to input their code manually to the computer using 1s and 0s, also got lazy. They decided it would be more fun to write their sequence of CPU instructions using mnemonics, such as CP for the "copy" instruction, MOV for the "move" instruction, CMP for the "compare" instruction, and so on. Then they wrote a program that converted mnemonic code to equivalent binary numbers, which could then be executed by the computer. With this, the **Assembly** (aka **ASM**) language was born.

A program written using these mnemonics is way more readable than its equivalent bunch of 1s and 0s. These early mnemonics and this programming style are both still widely used to this day. As modern CPUs support more complex instructions, more mnemonics were created, but the basic principle is still the same.

ASM is used to program systems such as an electronic microwave, or the computer system in a car. This programming style is also used on sections of code where extreme performance is needed, where saving even a few CPU cycles is relevant.

For example, imagine you are optimizing a high-performance web server and you've encountered a severe bottleneck. You can convert this bottleneck into ASM code, and inspect it. Many times we can modify the code to make it use fewer instructions. Lower level languages sometimes support the insertion of machine language within the programming language's normal code for implementing such fine optimizations. Writing in machine code gives you absolute control of what the CPU is actually doing when running your code.

STRUCTURED PROGRAMMING In the beginning, programs used GOTO commands to control the execution flow. This command makes the execution to jump to a different part of the code. As programs became more complex, it was nearly impossible to understand what a program did. Different possible flows of execution were all intertwined with GOTO and JUMP commands, in a condition known as *spaghetti code*.[3] In 1968, Dijkstra wrote his famous manifesto "GOTO Statement Considered Harmful", and it ushered a revolution. Code began to be separated in logical parts. Instead of ad-hoc

---

[3]If you want to curse someone else's source code, call it spaghetti code. 🍝

GOTOs, programmers began to use control structures (`if`, `else`, `while`, `for`...). That enabled programs to be much more easily written and debugged.

PROCEDURAL PROGRAMMING The next advance in the art of coding was procedural programming. It allows code to be organized into **procedures**, to avoid code replication and to increase code reusability. For instance, you can create a function that converts metric system measures to USA imperial units, and then call your function to reuse that same code whenever you want. This improved structured programming even further. Using procedures made it much easier to group related pieces of code, while separating them into different logical parts.

Declarative Programming

The **declarative programming paradigm** makes you state your desired result without dealing with every single intricate step that gets you there. It's about declaring *what* you want, and not *how* you want it done. In many scenarios, this allows programs to be much shorter and simpler. They are often also easier to read.

FUNCTIONAL PROGRAMMING In the functional programming paradigm, functions are more than just procedures. They're used to declare the relationship between two or more items, much like math equations. Functions are first-class citizens in the functional paradigm. They are treated the same way as any other primitive data type, such as strings and numbers.

Functions can receive other functions as arguments, and return functions as outputs. Functions that have these features are known as **higher-order functions**, because of their high expressive power. Many mainstream programming languages are incorporating such elements from the functional paradigm. You should take advantage of their marvelous expressiveness whenever possible.

For instance, most functional programming languages ship with a generic `sort` function. It can sort any sequence of items. The `sort` function accepts another function as input, that defines how items are compared in the sorting process. For example, let's say `coordinates` contains a list of geographical locations. Given two locations, the `closer_to_home` function says which is closer to your home. You could sort a list of locations by proximity to your home like this:

```
sort(coordinates, closer_to_home)
```

Higher-order functions are often used to filter data. Functional programming languages also offer a generic **filter** function, which receives a set of items to be filtered, and a filtering function that indicates if each item is to be filtered or not. For example, to filter out even numbers from a list, you can write:

```
odd_numbers ← filter(numbers, number_is_odd)
```

The `number_is_odd` is a function that receives a number and returns `True` if the number is odd, and `False` otherwise.

Another typical task that comes up when programming is to apply a special function over all items in a list. In functional programming, that is called **mapping**. Languages often ship with a built-in `map` function for this task. For example, to calculate the square of every number in a list, we can do this:

```
squared_numbers ← map(numbers, square)
```

The `square` is a function that returns the square of the number it's given. Map and filter occur so frequently, that many programming languages provide ways to write these expressions in simpler forms. For instance, in the Python programming language, you square numbers in a list a like this:

```
squared_numbers = [x**2 for x in numbers]
```

That's called a **syntactic sugar**: added syntax that lets you write expressions in simpler and shorter forms. Many programming languages provide several forms of syntactic sugar for you. Use them and abuse them.

Finally, when you need to process a list of values in a way that produces a single result, there's the `reduce` function. As input, it gets a list, an initial value, and a reducing function. The initial value will initiate an "accumulator" variable, which will be updated by the reducing function for every item in the list before it's returned:

```
function reduce(list, initial_val, func)
    accumulator ← initial_val
    for item in list
        accumulator ← func(accumulator, item)
    return accumulator
```

For example, you can use **reduce** to sum items in a list:

```
sum ← function(a, b): a + b
summed_numbers ← reduce(numbers, 0, sum)
```

Using **reduce** can simplify your code and make it more readable. Another example: if **sentences** is a list of sentences, and you want to calculate the total number of words in those sentences, you can write:

```
wsum ← function(a, b): a + length(split(b))
number_of_words ← reduce(sentences, 0, wsum)
```

The **split** function splits a string into a list of words, and the **length** function counts the number of items in a list.

Higher-order functions don't just receive functions as inputs— they can also produce new functions as outputs. They're even able to *enclose* a reference to a value into the function they generate. We call that a **closure**. A function that has a closure "remembers" stuff and can access the environment of its enclosed values.

Using closures, we can split the execution of a function which takes multiple arguments into more steps. This is called **currying**. For instance, suppose your code has this **sum** function:

```
sum ← function(a, b): a + b
```

The **sum** function expects two arguments, but it can be called with just one argument. The expression **sum(3)** doesn't return a number, but a new *curried* function. When invoked, it calls **sum**, using **3** as the first parameter. The reference to the value **3** got enclosed in the curried function. For instance:

```
sum_three ← sum(3)
print sum_three(1)   # prints "4".

special_sum ← sum(get_number())
print special_sum(1)   # prints "get_number() + 1".
```

Note that `get_number` will not be called and evaluated in order to create the `special_sum` function. A reference to `get_number` gets enclosed to `special_sum`. The `get_number` function is only called when we need to evaluate the `special_sum` function. This is known as **lazy evaluation**, and it's an important characteristic of functional programming languages.

Closures are also used to generate a set of related functions that follow a template. Using a function template can make your code more readable and avoid duplication. Let's see an example:

```
function power_generator(base)
    function power(x)
        return power(x, base)
    return power
```

We can use `power_generator` to generate different functions that calculate powers:

```
square ← power_generator(2)
print square(2)   # prints 4.

cube ← power_generator(3)
print cube(2)   # prints 8.
```

Note that the returned functions `square` and `cube` retain the value for the `base` variable. That variable only existed in the environment of `power_generator`, even though these returned functions are completely independent from the `power_generator` function. Again: a closure is a function that has access to some variables *outside* of its own environment.

Closures can also be use to manage a function's internal state. Let's suppose you need a function that accumulates the sum of all numbers that you gave it. One way to do it is with a global variable:

```
GLOBAL_COUNT ← 0
function add(x)
    GLOBAL_COUNT ← GLOBAL_COUNT + x
    return GLOBAL_COUNT
```

As we've seen, global variables should be avoided because they pollute the program's namespace. A cleaner approach is to use a closure to include a reference to the accumulator variable:

```
function make_adder()
    n ← 0
    function adder(x)
        n ← x + n
        return n
    return adder
```

This lets us create several adders without using global variables:

```
my_adder ← make_adder()
print my_adder(5) # prints 5.
print my_adder(2) # prints 7 (5 + 2).
print my_adder(3) # prints 10 (5 + 2 + 3).
```

PATTERN MATCHING Functional programming also allows you to treat functions like math functions. With math, we can write how functions behave according to the input. Notice the input pattern of the factorial function:

$$0! = 1,$$
$$n! = n \times (n - 1)!$$

Functional programming allows **pattern matching**—the process of recognizing that pattern. You can simply write:

```
factorial(0): 1
factorial(n): n × factorial(n - 1)
```

In contrast, imperative programming required you to write:

```
function factorial(n)
    if n = 0
        return 1
    else
        return n × factorial(n - 1)
```

Which one looks clearer? I'd go with the functional version whenever possible! Some programming languages are *strictly* functional; all the code is equivalent to purely mathematical functions. These languages go as far as being atemporal, with the order of the statements in the code not interfering in the code's behaviour. In these languages, all values assigned to variables are non-mutant. We call that **single assignment**. Since there is no program state, there is no point-in-time for the variable to change. Computing in a strict functional paradigm is merely a matter of evaluating functions and matching patterns.

Logic Programming

Whenever your problem is the solution to a set of logical formulas, you can use **logic programming**. The coder expresses logical assertions about a situation, such as the ones we saw in sec. 1.2. Then, queries are made to find out answers from the model that was provided. The computer is in charge of interpreting the logical variables and queries. It will also build a solution space from the assertions and search for query solutions that satisfy all of them.

The greatest advantage of the logical programming paradigm is that programming itself is kept to a minimum. Only facts, statements and queries are presented to the computer. The computer is in charge of finding the best way to search the solution space and present the results.

This paradigm isn't very well used in the mainstream, but if you find yourself working with artificial intelligence, natural language processing, remember to look into this.

Conclusion

As techniques for computer programming evolved, new programming paradigms emerged. They allowed computer code more expressiveness and elegance. The more you know of different programming paradigms, the better you'll be able to code.

In this chapter, we've seen how programming evolved from directly inputing 1s and 0s into the computer memory into writing assembly code. Then programming became easier with the establishment of control structures, such as loops and variables. We've seen how using functions allowed code to be better organized.

We saw some elements of the declarative programming paradigm that are becoming used in mainstream programming languages. And finally, we mentioned logic programming, which is the preferred paradigm when working in some very specific contexts.

Hopefully, you will have the guts to tackle any new programming language. They all have something to offer. Now, get out there and code!

Reference

- Essentials of Programming Languages, by Friedman

    - Get it at https://code.energy/friedman

- Code Complete, by McConnell

    - Get it at https://code.energy/code-complete

CONCLUSION

Computer science education cannot make anybody an
expert programmer any more than studying brushes
and pigment can make somebody an expert painter.

—ERIC S. RAYMOND

This book presented the most important topics of computer science
in a very simple form. It's the bare minimum a good programmer
should know about computer science.

I hope this new knowledge will encourage you to dig deeper
into the topics you like. That's why I included links to some of the
best reference books at the end of each chapter.

There are some important topics in computer science that are
notably absent from this book. How can you make computers in
a network covering the entire planet (the Internet) communicate
in a reliable way? How do you make several processors work in
synchrony to solve a computational task faster? One of the most
important programming paradigms, object-oriented programming,
also got left out. I plan to address these missing parts in a next book.

Also, you will have to write programs to fully learn what we've
seen. And that's a good thing. Coding can be unrewarding at first,
when you start learning how to do basic things with a programming language. Once you learn the basics, I promise it gets *super*
rewarding. So get out there and code.

Lastly, I'd like to say this is my first attempt at writing a book.
I have no idea how well it went. That's why your feedback about
this book would be incredibly valuable to me. What did you like
about it? Which parts were confusing? How do you think it could
be improved? Drop me a line at hi@code.energy.

APPENDIX

I Numerical Bases

Computing can be reduced to operating with numbers, because information is expressible in numbers. Letters can be mapped to numbers, so text can be written numerically. Colors are a combination of light intensities of red, blue and green, which can be given as numbers. Images can be composed by mosaics of colored squares, so they can be expressed as numbers.

Archaic number systems (e.g., roman numerals: I, II, III, ...) compose numbers from sums of digits. The number system used today is also based on sums of digits, but the value of each digit in position i is multiplied by d to the power of i, where d is the number of distinct digits. We call d the **base**. We normally use $d = 10$ because we have ten fingers, but the system works for any base d:

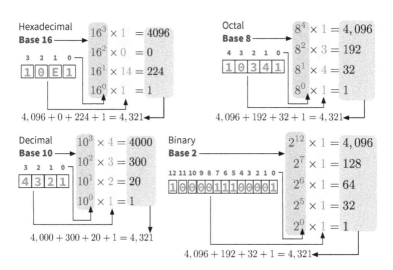

Figure 10.1   The number 4,321 in different bases.

II   Gauss' trick

The story goes that Gauss was asked by an elementary school teacher to sum all numbers from 1 to 100 as a punishment. To the teacher's amazement, Gauss came up with the answer 5,050 within minutes. His trick was to play with the order of elements of *twice* the sum:

$$2 \times \sum_{i=1}^{100} i = (1 + 2 + \cdots + 99 + 100) + (1 + 2 + \cdots + 99 + 100)$$

$$= \underbrace{(1 + 100) + (2 + 99) + \cdots + (99 + 2) + (100 + 1)}_{100 \text{ pairings}}$$

$$= \underbrace{101 + 101 + \cdots + 101 + 101}_{100 \text{ times}}$$

$$= 10,100.$$

Dividing this by 2 yields 5,050. We can formally write this reordering $\sum_{i=1}^{n} i = \sum_{i=1}^{n} (n + 1 - i)$. Thus:

$$2 \times \sum_{i=1}^{n} i = \sum_{i=1}^{n} i + \sum_{i=1}^{n} (n + 1 - i)$$

$$= \sum_{i=1}^{n} (i + n + 1 - i)$$

$$= \sum_{i=1}^{n} (n + 1).$$

There is no i in the last line, so $(n + 1)$ is summed over and over again n times. Therefore:

$$\boxed{\sum_{i=1}^{n} i = \frac{n(n + 1)}{2}.}$$

III Sets

We use the word **set** to describe a collection of objects. For example, we can call S the set of monkey face emoji:

$$S = \{🙊, 🙉, 🙈, 🙊\}.$$

SUBSETS A set of objects that is contained inside another set is called a **subset**. For example, the monkeys showing hands and eyes are $S_1 = \{🙈, 🙊\}$. All the monkeys in S_1 are contained in S. We write this $S_1 \subset S$. We can group monkeys showing hands and mouths in another subset: $S_2 = \{🙈, 🙊\}$.

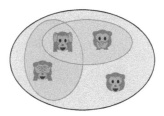

Figure 10.2 S_1 and S_2 are subsets of S.

UNION What monkeys belong to either S_1 or S_2? They are the monkeys in $S_3 = \{🙉, 🙈, 🙊\}$. This new set is called the **union** of the two previous sets. We write this $S_3 = S_1 \cup S_2$.

INTERSECTION What monkeys belong to both S_1 and S_2? They are the monkeys in $S_4 = \{🙈\}$. This new set is called the **intersection** of the two previous sets. We write this $S_4 = S_1 \cap S_2$.

POWER SETS Note that S_3 and S_4 are both still subsets of S. We also consider $S_5 = S$ and the empty set $S_6 = \{\}$ are both subsets of S. If you count all subsets of S, you will find $2^4 = 16$ subsets. If we see all these subsets as objects, we can also start to collect them into sets. The collection of all subsets of S is called its **power set**:

$$P_S = \{S_1, S_2, \ldots, S_{16}\}.$$

IV Kadane's Algorithm

In sec. 3.3, we introduced the Best Trade problem:

> BEST TRADE ⚒ You have the daily prices of gold for a interval of time. You want to find two days in this interval such that if you had bought then sold gold at those dates, you'd have made the maximum possible profit.

In sec. 3.7, we showed an algorithm that solves this in $\mathcal{O}(n)$ time and $\mathcal{O}(n)$ space. When Jay Kadane discovered it in 1984, he also showed how to solve the problem in $\mathcal{O}(n)$ time and $\mathcal{O}(1)$ space:

```
function trade_kadane(prices):
    sell_day ← 1
    buy_day ← 1
    B ← 1
    best_profit ← 0
    for each s from 2 to prices.length
        if prices[s] < prices[buy_day]
            B ← s
        profit ← prices[s] - prices[B]
        if profit ≥ best_profit
            sell_day ← s
            buy_day ← B
            best_profit ← profit
    return (sell_day, buy_day)
```

That's because we don't need to store the best buying day for every day of the input. We just need to store the best buying day relative to the best selling day found so far.